PATHWAYS

A Sourcebook of Options

By

Margaret Neylon

Attic Press

Dublin

First Published in 1991 by
Attic Press
4 Upper Mount Street
Dublin 2

British Library Cataloguing in Publication Data
Neylon, Margaret
    Pathways : a sourcebook of life options.
    I. Title
    824.914

    ISBN 1-85594-026-4

Cover Design: Sheila Naughton
Origination: Attic Press
Printing: The Guernsey Press Company Ltd.

CONTENTS

Dedication

To those who want to use more than 10 per cent of their mind

Margaret Neylon lives in Dublin where she is Creative Director of an advertising agency. A short story writer and playright, Margaret is the author of *The Wit and Wisdom of Women: A Thought Book* (1990) and co-compiler of *The Attic Book of Special Days* (1990) both published by Attic Press.

Introduction

Speaking from experience

From early childhood I have never really put my trust in doctors or medicaments, so much so that as a young child I used to pretend to take tablets while in fact I hid them under the bedroom carpet. Heaven knows what the subsequent owners of our family home thought when they came to put new floor coverings down! Still, although I never allowed a medical tablet down my throat when I was ill, here I am alive and well in mind and body. Somewhere inside I knew that my body had its own healing properties and that allowing a 'foreign body' into it would only unbalance its innate powers.

I first came to use a natural treatment when I wanted to give up smoking cigarettes. As a confirmed smoker for about fourteen years I had tried everything but the more my self-will said 'No' the more my body craved the nicotine. In despair I finally went to a hypnotherapist, feeling apprehensive and a bit sceptical! I had never met anyone who had used hypnotherapy before, but I was desperate. Before going in for my appointment I smoked what I hoped, yet did not quite believe, would be my last cigarette. From habit I left the open packet on the passenger seat of my car and went in for my session.

Two hours later, feeling more relaxed and rested than ever before, I went back to my car and saw the open cigarette pack on the seat. Instead of grabbing them and reaching for a light I calmly left the cigarettes lying there, as though they belonged to someone else. And that is how I felt! The hypnotherapist had implanted in my subconscious a certainty that from this point in time I was no longer 'a smoker'; when someone offered me a cigarette I could say 'No thank you, I don't smoke.' To my conscious mind this information seemed incredible. Of course I was a smoker. I had been one for fourteen years. The ads told me I was a smoker. The media said I would never give it up! Yet here I was, no longer a smoker. I wanted to accept this new information, and I did. I felt not the least pang of a withdrawal symptom. With the aid of hypnotic suggestion my mind had informed my body that I was a non-smoker, so why should I feel a withdrawal symptom?

At that visit to the hypnotherapist I lost my dependence on nicotine and found something that had been hidden from me before this: the enormous power of the mind. I slowly began to discover more about its potential.

When, a few years later, I began to suffer a skin complaint I first went to my doctor. She passed me on to a skin specialist. The specialist told me that, thankfully, I wasn't suffering from cancer but possibly from psoriasis. I was given a cream which worked for a short time, but whenever I felt under pressure from business or personal situations my skin would erupt again. It was an awful complaint, and I tried all sorts of things to rid myself of it, including various diets and a lot of creams and lotions. Most things worked for a short time but out of the blue the psoriasis would recur with a vengeance. I kept coming across books and articles which advised on 'How to live with Psoriasis'. My heart fell when I read this well-meaning advice. But I just wasn't willing to 'live' with it! So finally I decided to go back to my hypnotherapist.

Instead of suggesting potions and lotions he explained that the skin is 'the mirror of the mind', and that the mind controls the body. The one embryo from which each of us develops consists of the mind, the hormones and the skin, bone and organ structure. The mind sends messages via the hormones to the rest of the body. If my mind was in a confused state it would send confused messages to my nervous system and so my skin would not get the proper inner nourishment it needed. He then asked me if I was under stress in any area of my life. As it happened I was under stress in virtually every area at the time! Suddenly it all became clear to me why my skin was erupting. Things - and people - were literally 'getting under my skin'. With the help of hypnotherapy I practised self-hypnosis to enter into deep relaxation and control the messages from my brain to my body. Within six weeks my entire body was clear of psoriasis. I might add that I also changed my attitude towards the various problem areas of my life, again with the help of relaxation techniques learned in these sessions. On very rare occasions now I may get one small spot reappearing. This immediately activates me to return to self-hypnosis where I calm my mind and send the right messages to that part of my body where the complaint is showing itself. It works for me every time. For any other complaints I use the relaxation technique plus aromatherapy essences.

Allopathic (conventional) medicine

It is not generally known that medical practitioners of allopathy (the name for modern medicine) have to foreswear the practice of any other medicine. This originated from the time when pharmacists, particularly in Europe, laid pressure on governing bodies to actually outlaw such practices as homeopathy for the simple reason that these treatments required no 'compounding' by which the pharmacists made their living. (Homeopathy consists of one uncompounded remedy given in minute doses - there is no profit for the pharmacist there.) Other 'alternative' medicines suffered the same fate over the years, again for financial reasons. Because herbs could be grown in someone's garden and used in a home remedy, again the pharmacist would make no money from this form of medicine. We are told these forms of natural medicine do not work, yet today pharmaceutical companies take a natural herb, then spend millions developing a synthetic drug based on that herb's curative properties and sell it on the marketplace. Again, for the profit factor!

Holistic medicine

Today's medical doctors swear by the Hippocratic Oath on taking up medical practice, to endeavour to treat each 'patient' to the best of their ability. However, one very important belief of Hippocrates, the father of medicine, who lived and taught around 430 BC, was that both the psychological condition and the physical condition of the patient were to be taken into consideration if the correct remedy was to be found. This is almost completely overlooked by many members of today's medical profession, who hold that the body and the mind are two separate factors, and so teach methods of body healing only. To learn the workings of the mind, the student has to attend a school for psychology.

9

When I see how some of the medical profession write prescriptions which in effect suppress but never cure a patient's problem I feel like starting a revolution. I find it difficult to fathom the logic in prescribing such 'remedies' as Valium for unhappiness. It is tempting to believe that there's a worldwide conspiracy to keep people quiet at all costs in order to maintain the status quo and increase control! In a more tranquil moment, however, instead of starting a revolution I decided to write this book, to introduce some alternatives which can open up a new world to you - that of the limitless universe and of the power of your own mind. We typically use only about 10 per cent of our brain power. Just think of the potential of the remaining 90 percent!

Originally health and astrology were linked in holistic medicine. We were considered to be part of the whole universe, not separate from it. Following this philosopy, we would be affected by universal changes taking place at the time of our birth and throughout our life. Each part of our body would be under the influence of specific astrological signs; for example, women would be affected by the month's cycle of the moon. Hippocrates, believed that 'A physician without the knowledge of astrology has no right to call himself a physician.' Then in the early seventeenth century Culpepper wrote his *Complete Herbal* setting out each herb and its ruling planet. He believed that, for instance, the liver is ruled by Jupiter and that the herb dock is also ruled by the same planet. So if you were suffering from a liver complaint you would be treated with dock, which strengthens the liver. The important relationship between health and astrology lasted in the West until the eighteenth century when it collapsed with the advent of the scientific age.

If you are not quite convinced of predetermined astrological aspects, you may find it interesting to note the influences of the planets on our times, according to the astrological calendar. Those born between 1938-1957, for instance, are in positions of power at this time. A strong characteristic of this generation (who were born with the planet Pluto, the symbol of transformation, in the sign of Leo, the symbol of power and assertion,) is that they will not tolerate political power without popular consent. These were the students who rioted in the 1960s in France, the Civil Rights marchers in places as far apart as Alabama and Derry of the late 1960s, and the young Americans who refused to fight in Vietnam. Those born between

1943 and 1957 (with Neptune, the symbol of new awareness, in Libra, symbol of justice,) challenge the social and sexual mores laid down by earlier generations. Such are the women who founded the women's movement and fought for equality. Little wonder there was the social and sexual revolution of the 1960s and 1970s! Note, however, that those born after 1957 will be much more conservative but will be interested in the occult (Neptune in Scorpio, symbol of depth of thought and hidden knowledge), and in improving the ecology and quality of life for everyone. (Pluto in Virgo, the symbol of perfection). This will tie in with the character of the Age of Aquarius when science goes hand in hand with intuition.

Now that we are in the early part of the Age of Aquarius a lot of barriers will be coming down, not just in the political arena, as we have seen in very recent times. The open and inquiring mind which is typified in the Aquarian will mix intellect and intuition with science and technology in the hope of making a better world.

A balance of mind and body

When I write about dis-ease I hyphenate it because in holistic medicine, which treats the whole person, not just the body, good health is brought about by the balance of mind and body. This can be achieved ony when the mind is at ease with itself. Where there is disharmony in the mind it will create dis-ease in the person. To heal the body we must therefore heal the mind.

Oriental medical philosophy believes that the body contains energy, known as Ch'i, which is a balance of Yin and Yang, positive and negative energy, neither of which can exist in isolation from the other. Again physical and mental health is a matter of harmony and balance.

A new enthusiasm

At about the same time I was treating myself with the aid of hypnosis I met friends with whom I had not been in contact for some years. We discovered that during those intervening years we had all become involved in some way in these 'alternative beliefs': self-healing, homeopathy, acupuncture, tarot, astrology.

We must have found friendship with one another through some unknown bond, and been predestined to meet again when we were more mature.

I also discovered, from talking about my interest in these areas, that people I had worked with for years had also been interested in alternative pathways but had never brought up the subject in case they would be thought eccentric in some way. I find this quite often. However, being an Aquarian Snake (see the characteristics of these signs in the two chapters on Astrology), I am rarely held back by public opinion, so I tend to throw a pebble in the pond and watch for the ripples.

When I was talking with my friends I noticed that one might be an expert in say, tarot reading, but know little about astrology, while an astrologer might know all about that subject but nothing about palmistry. Another might be a herbalist but be ignorant about self-healing, and so on. I became interested in all these subjects yet could find no one book which covered them all in any detail. So that is why I have brought them together between the two covers.

I am not an expert in all of these different life options but I am an enthusiast, and I hope *Pathways* will encourage you to become interested enough in some of these subjects to find out more. After each chapter you will find a brief list of further reading matter on each subject and of course your telephone directory will give you names and addresses of specialists in your own area. I hope that, like me, this new knowledge will help to fulfil the potential that is within you and also help you enjoy life and the universe to the full.

Divining by Tarot

When you look at the Tarot deck you may find their pictorial designs a little mysterious and sinister at first glance. However, Tarot cards are simply tools used by adepts to divine hidden information from the images and symbols of each card. All are highly detailed and full of mystical symbolism and it is from this that a reader interprets the meaning of a spread.

Some use the Tarot to give a life reading on a subject similar to a natal chart that is drawn up by an astrologer, but there are several different 'spreads' possible for different types of readings. Where Tarot cards really stand apart though is in their ability to give answers to specific questions about a person's choices on all sorts of topics from career, to purchases, to relationships.

A brief background to the Tarot

No one is certain when or where Tarot cards were first developed, but we do know that they have been in existence for many hundreds of years. Some believe that the Tarot goes back to ancient Egyptian rites, some that they originated in China, others in India. It is often said that the Major Arcana and the Minor Arcana originated as two separate decks, and that the latter were developed in the area of Italy around the River Taro. The most likely answer is that they were developed over a number of years and throughout a number of countries by gypsies migrating to Western Europe who made their living from their ability to read people's fortunes.

Over the centuries Tarot reading has come in and out of fashion, and been applauded and banned by rulers and Churches. Its most famous revival happened at the turn of the twentieth century when some members of London 'society', including the poet WB Yeats and the occultist Aleister Crowley, joined The Hermetic Order of the Golden Dawn, who studied and wrote about the mysticism of the Tarot.

Some notes on reading the Tarot

If you are interested in developing your skills as a Tarot reader you will find that there are many different designs available, from the ornate 1910 design conceived by the occult writer AE Waite and drawn by Pamela Coleman Smith, to the more art noveau designs of the Aquarian Tarot. The choice of design is yours, but they should be treated with respect, and used only for Tarot purposes. Handle them with care and do not encourage others to use them unless they are shuffling them for a reading.

When undertaking a reading for another person, remember that the person will take what you say seriously, no matter how much nonchalance is shown. While you may talk easily about something negative which has happened in the past, a negative show for the future should be toned down.

The Tarot deck

The Tarot deck consists of 78 cards. There are 22 key cards, known as the Major Arcana, and the remaining 56 cards are known as the Minor Arcana. The Minor Arcana are divided into four suits of fourteen cards each.

There is plenty of literature available for those interested in finding out more about the Tarot, and the following is just a brief description of the meanings of the Major and Minor Arcana. When reading, some cards may be placed upside-down (reversed). Depending on the deck and/or the reader, reversed cards may be interpreted as a diluted version of the upright meaning, the opposite of the upright meaning, or can be treated as though they are upright.

The Major Arcana
These have a powerful imagery and the 22 key cards can, and often are, used separately for a reading. The word Arcana means mystery or secret, so these cards show major changes and events in the questioner's life. The following descriptions are based on

those conceived by AE Waite in 1910, with a basic interpretation on each.

0 The Fool
Depicts a young person stepping into the unknown, carrying a bundle over the shoulder, a white rose and a confident smile.
Interpretation: The beginning of something new (new job/new home/new relationship). Unlimited choices. Innocence and enthusiasm.

I The Magician
Depicts a strong, handsome young man standing over a table on which are placed the four suits of the Minor Arcana. He holds a wand aloft. Above his head is the symbol for infinity, the lemniscate.
Interpretation: Creativity and intellect. Skill and dexterity. Diplomacy and self-confidence. It is the beginning of a new cycle and new opportunities abound.

II The High Priestess
A dark haired young woman seated between two pillars marked B for Boaz (negation) and J for Jachin (beginning). On her lap she holds a scroll.
Interpretation: The priestess indicates intuition and common sense. She stands for ancient knowledge and scholarship, honesty and integrity.

III The Empress
A blonde woman sits outdoors surrounded by water, trees and ripening wheat. She wears a crown made of stars and beside her is a shield bearing the symbol of Venus.
Interpretation: Abundance, material gain, fertility, wealth and contentment. Physical love, the fruition of projects, a beneficial move.

IV The Emperor
A stern bearded man sits on a throne with an orb in one hand, a staff in the other, signifying life and immortality.
Interpretation: Power and influence, security and respect. Supportive and stable. An older person who can be relied on. Steady progress in career.

V The Hierophant
A pope seated on his throne, hand raised in blessing, with two supplicants kneeling at his feet.

Interpretation: Conformity, spiritual kindness and mercy. Use tried and tested means to achieve your goals. Listen to the wisdom of older people.

VI The Lovers
Adam and Eve in the Garden of Eden beside the Tree of Life and the Tree of Knowledge, with the Archangel and the Sun looking down on them.
Interpretation: Love blossoming, harmony between friends. Also a choice to be made between two alternatives in love, business or a course of action.

VII The Chariot
A young armoured man driving a chariot drawn by two sphinx, in the background is a walled city.
Interpretation: Indicates struggle, but hard work will bring triumph over adversity in matters to do with money, people, health and home. Can also indicate good news about a vehicle.

VIII Strength
A woman clothed in white, a crown of flowers and a garland about her waist, with the lemniscate of infinity above her head, touches a lion gently.
Interpretation: Strength to overcome health problems and life obstacles with gentle perseverance and fortitude. Mind over matter.

IX The Hermit
A hooded monk stands on top of a mountain with a staff in one hand and in the other, a lantern from which shines a star.
Interpretation: Stand alone and reflect with prudence and caution. Accept advice from an older, wiser person. Meditate for inner enlightenment.

X The Wheel of Fortune
The Wheel of Fortune suspended in the sky with the symbols of mercury, sulphur, salt and water in the centre, the sphinx atop it and Anubis, symbolising final judgement, on its right. To its left is the snake and at each corner the four beasts of the Apocalypse.
Interpretation: A change is signified, usually a turn for the better. Grasp an unforeseen opportunity. Karma, that which you give out, comes back to you.

XI Justice
Justice, with a sword upraised in her right hand, a scale held in

her left. She sees everything which takes place before her.
Interpretation: Justice and fairness in all matters including legal problems and business partnerships. Harmony in relationships. Clear vision.

XII The Hanged Man
A young man hangs suspended from a tree, a golden aura about his head, a happy contemplative smile on his face.
Interpretation: A gradual reversal in circumstances and attitudes when time will seem suspended as one changes from the material world to the appreciation of the spiritual. Self-sacrifice is required to achieve this goal.

XIII Death
Death, a skeleton, rides a white horse. He is surrounded by a praying bishop, a woman and a child and there is a dead king at his feet. In the background is a ship in sail and a rising or descending sun.
Interpretation: Renewal through renaissance. Death of the old self to make way for the new. Freedom through change. Sometimes political unrest.

XIV Temperance
A winged angel, one foot on land, one on water, pouring the contents of a cup in one hand into cup in the other. Surrounded by flowers and a fertile countryside.
Interpretation: Balance and harmony. Peace and relaxation. Spiritual comfort. A mix of proper proportions after a time of stress in family, business and health matters.

XV The Devil
A winged and horned devil, his right hand raised in a sign of black magic and his left holding a torch downwards, overlooks a man and woman who are chained in bondage.
Interpretation: Bondage to the material triumphs over spirituality. Evil can result from wrong decisions and irresponsible behaviour. Repression will continue unless you move to break the bonds. Sexual problems may arise.

XVI The Tower
A tower has been struck by lightning and is aflame. A crown which has been atop it is now dislodged and two figures are toppling down.
Interpretation: Calamity and loss. Illusions shattered. Beliefs

destroyed. Punishment for pride.

XVII The Star

A young blonde woman kneels at the shoreline, pouring water from two jugs into the earth and the water. One foot on land, one on water, she is surrounded by a large 8-pointed star and several smaller ones. A bird sings in a tree behind her.

Interpretation: Insight and inspiration. The star of hope, faith and optimism. Good fortune awaits. New horizons. New enterprises will succeed. An interest in education and the occult.

XVIII The Moon

A dog and a wolf howl at the moon which shows its face full and crescent. A lobster crawls from a pool whose source winds from a distant horizon, passing between two watch towers.

Interpretation: The dog represents the domesticated, the wolf the wild aspect of our mind, the lobster the subconscious. Mysterious, female aspect of things. Uncertainty and sometimes disarray. Channel your imagination towards artistry. Develop your occult powers.

XIX The Sun

A young, happy child rides a horse, carrying a red banner and surrounded by flowers. The sun shines down on the scene.

Interpretation: Joy and happiness, success and good health. All goals achieved. All efforts rewarded. Happy marriage, unselfish love. Youthful fun.

XX Judgement

A man, woman and child raise their arms in welcome at the angel emerging from the clouds who blows the last trumpet.

Interpretation: Spiritual and material combine in harmony. Clear evaluation of past events and rewards. The ending of a phase, the ending of a duty. A clear conscience.

XXI The World

A naked woman, holding a rod in each hand, dances within a wreath of leaves. The angel, eagle, lion and bull of the Apocalypse are in each corner.

Interpretation: A turning point. A new life. The chance to look back and survey a job well done, the fulfilment of all desires. Freedom, rewards. Inner enlightenment and peace.

The Minor Arcana

These are carefully illustrated to symbolise the meanings of each card, but do not have quite such strong imagery as the Major Arcana. As the name suggests, these foretell minor events in the questioner's life.

There are four suits of cards: Coins, Cups, Staves and Swords .

Coins: Also known as Pentacles. Coins refer to money, property, status and the organisation of work and business.

Cups: Indicate matters of romance, marriage, love, creativity, education, intuition and material possessions.

Staves: Also known as Wands and Rods, these indicate work, business, legal and family business matters. Also refer to overseas travel, property dealings and the home.

Swords: Indicate courage, authority, sadness, betrayal, trouble and action to be taken quickly.

Court Cards

Kings and Queens: Represent men (Kings) and women (Queens) of authority and wisdom, 35 years plus. Lovers, friends, relatives, colleagues. Presently already in the questioner's life, or coming into it.

Knights: Represent young men, often lovers, friends, relatives or colleagues, as well as the lessening of the importance of an older man in the questioner's life.

Pages: The impact young women or children, a messenger, a friend will have on the questioner at the time of the reading.

The meanings of the suits of cards
Coins: *Interpretation*

Ace	Good news about money through a promotion, a lucky win or a bonus.
2	Division of property, too many demands being made on questioner.
3	Material gains through successful skills, home purchase or home improvements.
4	Long term financial stability on the way.
5	Financial loss possible while finding love and affection from an unlikely source.

6	Sharing out of your money received from a large cash injection, and you can afford to be benevolent.
7	Keep up the hard work; you are building firm foundations for future growth.
8	Invest time in perfecting a new skill which will advance your career in the future.
9	Material gain and success. Domestic circumstances improve.
10	Great personal achievement and financial reward. The future looks good.
Page	Good news about money and business travel. A young person may make you feel proud.
Knight	Travel and business look good. A young person will bring good news.
Queen	A business woman who is skilled and honest will help in negotiations. She would be a good companion and bring security.
King	A tough, reliable business man who doesn't take risk; can be of help to the family.

Cups: *Interpretation*

Ace	Start of a loving association. Lifetime partnership or marriage, long-term friendship, birth.
2	The successful outcome of two people getting together, in love or in business.
3	Reason for celebration, whether a wedding, a birth or perhaps a housewarming.
4	Pleasure can be enjoyed if the questioner will only recognise it when it is found.
5	Loss of pleasure, and regret for its loss. There is still something left from which to build happiness, however.
6	Contact old friends or family members; return to your roots to build for the future.
7	May be blinded by illusion and too much choice, so take time to make far-reaching decisions.
8	The situation may be bad at the moment but with courage and patience things will begin to improve.
9	Reason for inner pride, which should not be flaunted. May refer to material success.
10	Whatever success you desire will be yours.
Page	A time for reflection and perhaps study. Where business is concerned take time to make decisions.

Knight   Changes may happen in your romantic life, with the coming or going of someone who cares for you.

Queen   A female friend who is maternal will give you love and comfort, but she may be too demanding in return.

King   A male friend who may be somewhat possessive and unreliable, cares for you and will bring you happiness.

Rods: *Interpretation*

Ace   Good news will soon be communicated through the post or over the phone. Also heralds the birth of a child, or the birth of a new project.

2   A good property deal can be struck if you beware the competition.

3   The beginning of a new job or a new relationship or partnership. Travel and communication will be successful.

4   A feeling of security. An investment in property.

5   Some problems arising with travel and negotiations. Keep up your courage and things will work out.

6   Victory in negotiations, legal matters and agreements.

7   Take time and patience to work out problems caused by opposition.

8   By broadening your horizons you may find new friendship, if not love.

9   You are secure at the moment so don't take chances which may upset this. Be prudent and stay put for the present.

10   You may find yourself oppressed in some manner at work or at home by more responsibility being thrust upon you.

Page   Energetic movement, meetings and greetings. Minor property matters will work out.

Knight   Change of place and change of faces. Pleasant dealings with a young man.

Queen   A good business woman, alert, charming and fun, who should work in partnership in order to succeed.

King   A friendly, charming and extrovert man who is a good friend will prove a boon to the questioner.

Swords: *Interpretation*

Ace   A difficult but rewarding project. Some sort of medical treatment. Power and justice. A new passion.

2	There is little change in your circumstances within the near future. A settlement will be reached in a contentious matter.
3	A piercing to the heart, through a breakup of a relationship or a sad occasion.
4	Good news if you've been ill, for this refers to recovery. You may need to recuperate alone from a stressful situation.
5	A breakup of a loving relationship, a violent argument, jealousy against you.
6	Movement away from strife, and travel over water. Possible visitor from afar.
7	Sort out any problems by decisive action even if it means cutting your losses.
8	You may feel trapped and helpless in your present situation. Don't force change; it will come in time.
9	This can refer to illness in the questioner, or the effect illness in someone close will have on the questioner.
10	Watch out for a stab in the back or a sudden, unlooked for change. Problems may arise in work, in marriage, in general situation.
Page	Something interesting is on the way, in your business or your social life. Stay alert for a beneficial opportunity arising.
Knight	Swift changes will occur and swift decisions will need to be made. An intelligent young man will have some influence in your life.
Queen	A clever but detached woman who demands respect will help the questioner on a professional level.
King	A tough professional man without humour will bring problems which the questioner will have to deal with. If it is a financial problem, he will help the questioner.

Making a correct spread

It is important that a reading should be carried out in comfort and on a table or surface where there is plenty of room. The questioner has a choice of dozens of differing spreads, each giving different readings. In all cases the reader and the questioner may be either the same or different persons.

When preparing for a reading bear the following points in

mind:

1. After shuffling the cards a little, the reader should pass them on to the questioner who shuffles them again, then cuts the deck into three piles with the left hand (that closest to the heart).

2. The reader should then pick up the three piles of cards in the opposite order to which they were placed, ie the pile that was put down last becomes the pile the reader picks up first.

3. When spreading the cards, the reader should turn the cards from their side on to the surface used. In other words, do not turn from top to bottom because this will reverse cards incorrectly.

4. A reading can be done using only the Major Arcana or by mixing both Major and Minor Arcanas. The choice is yours.

Examples of simple spreads
The Six Card Spread
Choose six important areas of the questioner's life, and make a note of them. For this example the questioner could take:
* The present situation
* Matters relating to love and family
* Financial matters
* Career matters
* Health matters
* Property and home

Shuffle and cut the cards as directed above, then pick up each of the first six cards from its side and place beside each other.

The reading will make a story which should be recognisable to the questioner.

The short spread
For a quicker reading the questioner can decide on a reading for just two areas, in which case the reader notes which areas are chosen, then picks up two cards which are placed beside each other. When reading the symbolism of these two cards, another card can be placed on top of these two to get a clearer reading.

The Yes or No reading
For a fast answer to an important question, the questioner shuffles as before, then the cards are laid face down on the table. Three cards are chosen from this and are placed face up. The

following is the answer to the question:

* All three cards right side up = Yes.
* Two cards only right side up = Yes, with qualifications.
* Two cards reversed = No.
* All cards reversed = Definitely no!

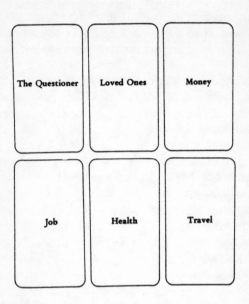

The Celtic Cross
This is the most popular and well-known spread and can give quite a detailed reading; it is the one most likely to answer a given question.

Before shuffling the cards, the reader must choose a card most suitable to the questioner. This card is called the Significator. A Court Card is normally chosen; for example the Queen of Coins would refer to a questioner who is a woman involved in business, perhaps running her own company; the King of Cups would signify a man involved in the arts or education; a Page of Coins could signify a woman who is an employee of a company. The card chosen as Significator should be kept separate.

Prepare for a spread as before, then lay the cards out as follows:

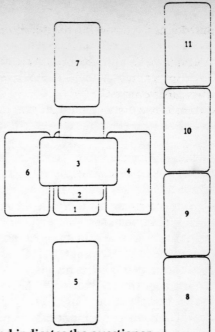

Card 1: The Significator
This is placed down first and indicates the questioner.
Card 2: The Present Situation
This is placed on top of Card 1 and indicates what is currently influencing the questioner most.
Card 3: Opposing Forces
This is placed sideways on Cards 1 and 2, and shows the person or circumstances opposing the questioner.
Card 4: The Goal
This is placed above Cards 1, 2 and 3 and indicates the most that can be achieved under present circumstances.
Card 5: The Background
Placed beneath Cards 1, 2 and 3, this tells the background of the situation and hidden circumstances.
Card 6: The Recent Past
Placed to the left of Cards 1, 2 and 3, this tells of the recent past or a recent development.
Card 7: The Near Future
Placed to the right of Cards 1, 2 and 3, this indicates people or developments which will come about in the near future.
Card 8: The Seeker
This is placed at the far right of Card 5, forming the base of a new column of cards. Card 8 tells of the questioner and the next step in the questioner's life.

25

Card 9: The Environment
Placed above Card 8, this tells of the people or situation surrounding the questioner at present.
Card 10: Place above Card 9, this indicates the inner secrets and fears of the questioner.
Card 11: Placed above Card 10, this indicates the outcome of the overall situation and the answer to the question.

When reading this more complex spread, bear in mind the following: If there are many cards from the Major Arcana, this indicates that there are forces at work in the situation outside the questioner's control. If there are a large number of the same suit in the spread, then keep these in mind. A number of Swords can mean strife and loss, a number of Cups can mean emotion, artistry and friendship. If the final card, No. 10, is ambiguous, it can indicate that there is no answer forthcoming at the moment, or the reader can take the next Major Arcana card from the pack and use this as the outcome.

With practice and intuition the reader can learn to read an entire story from the spread. There are many more to choose from, some of which are related to numerology, some to astrology.

Where to find out more

Waite, AE, *Key to the Tarot*, Rider & Company, England, 1982.
Sharman-Burke, Juliet and Liz Green, *The Mythic Tarot*, Simon & Shuster, New York, 1986.
Kaplan, Stuart R , *Tarot Cards for Fun & Fortune Telling*, Aquarian Publishing Co. England, 1978.
Fenton, Sasha (Ed), *The Aquarian Book of Fortune Telling*, Aquarian Press, England, 1987.

Herbalism

Have you ever wondered at nature's intent when she gave us so many plants and flowers in so many shapes and sizes? What we in this century call a weed is, in fact, a flower or plant which has gone to seed. Not too many years ago the dandelion, nettle, bramble and camomile were prized for their curative powers. According to herbalists, each has its own raison d'être which is to heal and cure animal and human.

If you live in close proximity to animals you probably have noticed how they automatically sense the correct thing to eat when they are not well. A cat or dog will chew a long blade of grass which will help them regurgitate their stomach contents, an animal suffering snake bite will chew the snake root, another with a fever will sit in solitude by a water source, relaxed and with enough liquid to quench thirst. Animals have an inbred knowledge of nature's answer to illness and they need nothing but nature to cure it.

The philosopy behind herbalism

Herbalism is, simply, health from plants. Unlike allopathy, or orthodox medicine, which attacks the germs or toxins in the body alone, the philosophy of herbalism is similar to that of homeopathy and other treatments such as traditional Chinese medicine. In the event of dis-ease in an individual the solution from these natural methods is to stimulate the life force inherent in the body so that it can fight back to remedy itself. A herbalist will therefore prescribe minute doses of specific herbal cures in order to allow the life force to regain its harmony over a period of time.

A short history of herbalism

The Great Herbal of China, *Pen Tsao*, which lists about 1,000 herbal remedies, was written around the year 3,000 BC, and there is plenty of evidence that herbs were used to treat dis-ease in Ancient Egypt, Babylonia and Assyria up to 1,500 years BC. Herbalism was the medicine of the Romans and Pliny the Elder wrote a classic *Natural History*, which taught that there was a herbal remedy for every complaint.

When Nicholas Culpepper wrote *English Physician and Complete Herbal* in the seventeenth century ad, he linked herbs with their astrological influence (ie their effect would be based on the influence of their planet). This belief held true for a further century but, when interest in astrology waned with the advent of the scientific age a hundred years or so later, so did belief in herbal cures.

In this century it has again been recognised that herbs have helpful healing, cosmetic or digestive properties and even the major allopathic drug companies now use extracts from herbs or else manufacture synthetic extracts themselves.

How it works

Herbs do not tend to give immediate cures as they are taken to enhance the power of the life force (*vix medicatrix naturae*) and obviously it takes a little while to bring it into balance again. In fact, with this in mind, a herbalist is more likely to not only treat a patient suffering from dis-ease but will also give a remedy which will enable the patient to remain in good health by keeping this life force in proper balance. Therefore do not expect overnight miracles if you use herbal remedies, but take them on a daily basis as an addition to your usual diet and your body will then be fitter to protect you from dis-ease. For instance, alternate one cup of tea a day with a herbal tea, and add herbs to your meals.

Some herbal cures

Elderflower tea is a good tonic medicine for daily consumption, and is also used as a remedy for chills and colds. **Marigold tea**

made from the petals aids intestinal disorders. A **hawthorn infusion** made from flowers and dried haws treats high and low blood pressure and can also act as a treatment for insomnia. **Lime flower** infusion is another aid for insomnia and nervous disorders. **Lady's Mantle** helps the menstrual cycle and **Yarrow tea** is good for remedying colds, while it also helps in menopausal problems.

The Romans gave **wild thyme** to melancholic people, and an infusion relieves headaches due to excess of alcohol. **Camomile**, revered by the Egyptians and dedicated to their gods, is known as 'the plants' physician' because its presence in a garden will improve the health of its neighbours, while camomile tea is well known as a delicious soothing sedative. The druids held **meadowsweet** to be sacred and an infusion acts as a good treatment for rheumatism, arthritis and oedema.

Herbs such as **rosemary** (treats headaches, nervous and digestive disorders and rejuvenates the hair and skin) can be used in every-day cooking to enhance the taste of foods such as lamb and fish. **Sage** purifies the blood and stops unhealthy perspiration. Sage is used in stuffings and cooked with pork and goose, and can be used in sandwiches or made into a refreshing tea.

The **potato** can cure many complaints. Raw potato juice is a cure for stomach ulcers and also diabetes. Grated raw potato can be used as a poultice to relieve burns, sunburn and also chilblains. For those who suffer from migraine and headache, place a slice of fresh raw potato on each temple to gain relief.

The **daisy** has many uses. Chewing the fresh daisy leaf will help cure mouth ulcers. The fresh leaves can be included in a salad to give it added flavour, or they can be served cooked with various meats. As an infusion, the daisy cleans the blood and therefore clears up skin problems, while it also eases the respiratory tract.

Herbal teas

Herbal teas and tisanes are made usually by adding leaves, seeds or dried flowers or berries to boiling water as one makes Indian or China tea. Sweeten teas with honey if necessary, and only add milk if advised in the recipe.

Whichever recipe you wish to use it is always important to

follow instructions carefully, especially if choosing herbs yourself, and never take a chance picking something you are not quite certain about. If you wish to experiment, buy herbs or tea-bags from a health store and to enjoy them at their best make sure they have been freshly packed. When using fresh herbs bruise them or tear them a little before adding water and this will enable the goodness to come out. A tea cure should be taken consistently for 3-4 weeks. Never use a metal teapot when making herbal teas, and leave to infuse for the time instructed only; if it is left over-long or under-long this can give the opposite effect to the one required.

Herbal teas or tisanes (French for 'nourishing concoction') are health giving and are used, especially on the Continent, as a helpful addition to the diet on a daily basis. Some tisanes can be used for therapeutic purposes, others for beauty. Some recipes involve a mixture of many herbs, others use flower petals or leaves from such plants as mint or seeds.

An Infusion is made by adding water which is either boiling, warm or cold to herbal flowers and leaves. Decoction entails boiling and simmering the coarser flowers and leaves in water. A maceration involves soaking, boiling and simmering and is used for the hard parts of a herb or plant such as bark, roots and hard leaves.

Herbal dishes

The following are some examples of herbs used in everyday cooking with a brief explanation of their healing properties:

Dill, whose name originates from the Norse 'Dilla' which means 'to lull', is an important digestive. Dill seeds were once known as 'Meeting House Seeds' because people would take them before going to church in order to dull their appetite. Dill is also used in baby's gripe water in order to aid digestion.

In cookery dill leaves or seeds (the latter are more pungent) are used for enhancing a food's flavour. Dill is particularly popular in fish, meat and poultry dishes, salad and salad dressings and as a substitute for salt in sandwiches.

Nasturtiums (Capucines), will grow almost anywhere and their scarlet and yellow flowers and bright green heart-shaped leaves give a startling dash of colour to hedges, walls, window boxes and herb gardens. The flowers, leaves and seeds can be eaten, and each has a hot, peppery taste, the seeds being the strongest in flavour. Nasturtiums are a great source of Vitamin C and also have strong therapeutic values as an antibiotic. In German speaking countries especially nasturtiums are valued for this. Flu symptoms are also helped by eating finely chopped nasturtium leaves which will reduce such complaints as sore throats, aches in joints and headaches. The flowers, leaves and seeds can be used to add a peppery flavour to salads; chopped leaves can be added to spreads and sandwiches, and seeds to flavour sauces.

Rosemary, 'that's for remembrance' according to Ophelia in Hamlet, and such a belief was handed down through the centuries from the Greeks whose students wore it to strengthen the memory. Both the leaves and flowers can be used in cooking or in making tea, wine or liqueur to stimulate the circulation and help a weak digestion.

Boil rosemary in water and use as a skin tonic, and wash hair in this water to stimulate hair growth. Rosemary adds a delicious flavour to poultry, fish and game dishes, and gives a subtle flavour to fruit salads and cold cider cup.

Wild garlic produces an essential oil containing Vitamin C among other things and shares the same highly prized properties as the cultivated garlic, acting as an antibiotic and antiseptic, curing hypertension, sciatica and gout, and stimulating the liver and cleansing the circulation.

Herbs for beauty

Some herbs have a wonderful effect on the body externally, and can be used as oil, ointments, as face packs and compresses, in the bath as liquid additive or as 'pochettes' (little bags made from material such as muslin filled with herbs and hung under the hot water tap) to enrich and enliven the skin.

Valerian will help aid sleep, a bath of **camomile, rosemary** and **horsetail** will soothe the nervous system, while **peppermint** or **pine needles** are advised for skin troubles, as will a **blackberry leaves** face pack.

A compress of **dandelion leaves** will improve the circulation of the face and clear it of impurities. A cold water compress of **sage, lady's mantle** or **peppermint** will tone up the skin and reduce large pores.

There are herb remedies for improving the eyes: for example eyebright, used as a compress or bath, an infusion of elder flower water, again used as a compress or bath and camomile, used as a cold compress.

Hair tonics are made from a mixture of such herbs as lime flowers, nettle, camomile, horsetail, yarrow and rosemary. These can stimulate new growth and act as a tonic to brighten or lighten the hair.

There are many health shops where you can receive good advice and recipes for making your own herbal remedies, or choose pre-packed goods which you can try. When taken as directed herbs are a soothing, enjoyable remedy free from harm.

Where to find out more

Grieve, M ,*A Modern Herbal*, Penguin Books, England, 1970.
Lowenfeld, Claire and Philippa Back, *Herbs for Health and Cookery*, Pan Books, London, 1965.
Culpeper, Nicholas, *Complete Herbal*, Omega Books, London, 1985.

Shiatsu

The word 'Shiatsu' is the Japanese for 'finger pressure'. It is a form of massage which applies manual and digital pressure to the skin in order to stimulate or sedate the energy balance of Yin and Yang, known as Ki in Japan and as Ch'i in China.

A short history of Shiatsu

Forms of acupuncture and acupressure have been used in Japan for hundreds of years. Shiatsu itself was founded by the Japanese Tokujiro Namikoshi in the early part of the twentieth century. While trying to relieve the acute pain his mother was suffering, Tokujiro Namikoshi discovered that by massaging certain reflexes and meridians in the body Ki could be rebalanced, bringing relief from pain and revitalising the body's innate healing powers. In 1925 Tokujiro Namikoshi founded his own Institute in Japan for teaching this healing method and Shiatsu is now a widely recognised form of treatment. It is becoming increasingly more popular in Europe and North America as well as in Japan, of course.

The philosophy behind Shiatsu

Shiatsu is seen by the Japanese as a way of life rather than just a cure for illness. It not only helps the healing process by stimulating or sedating Ki, it also revitalises the body's inner curative powers, with the intention of developing bodies which are capable of resisting sickness. The therapist takes a holistic view in treating a person through Shiatsu. Therefore the person's lifestyle, attitudes and diet are taken into account when a diagnosis is undertaken. While Shiatsu is used to overcome disease of the body and mind, people also undergo sessions in order to enhance their lives. For instance, as a session of Shiatsu re-energises the body and mind it is often given before an important task is undertaken, and following that task another session then relaxes a person.

How Shiatsu works
It was Tokujiro Namikoshi's intention that a person should not suffer any discomfort while being given a Shiatsu session. Therefore, the therapist uses fingers and hands to gently palpitate the skin areas at specific reflexes and meridians in order to diagnose any disharmony; then the pressure is increased gradually. The skin areas used to treat reflexes and meridians in Shiatsu massage are different than those used for acupuncture or acupressure in traditional Chinese medicine.

Shiatsu is a holistic treatment and the therapist will make four types of diagnosis in order to carry out a correct treatment on each person.

Bo-Shin Diagnosis
Bo-Shin is a visual diagnosis. Here the therapist will study body language, attitude, posture and energy levels. Central to the philosophy of Shiatsu is the awareness that the microcosm (the face) reflects the macrocosm (the body); in other words the face is the mirror-image of the body. Therefore a study of the eyes, the skin and the tongue will give a lot of information on the health of a person being treated.

Mon-Shin Diagnosis
Mon-Shin is the querying diagnosis. The therapist will need to discover a person's past medical history as well as her present lifestyle and diet.

Setsu-Shin Diagnosis
Setsu-Shin is the diagnosis of touch. A study of the muscle tone and the skin's flexibility will tell the therapist about the balance of energy in the person.

With improved circulation will come an improvement in the digestive function, which in turn will enhance the skin and muscle tone, with the end result that a person will look younger.

Bun-Shin Diagnosis
The fourth is a diagnosis of the senses. The therapist will use

personal skill and intuition to diagnose a person's health by smell and hearing. For instance a high, excited voice or a low, hesitant tone will give the therapist an insight into the balance of a person's Ki.

A Shiatsu session

A session of Shiatsu will last for between 50-60 minutes. When attending a therapist make sure you wear loose clothing and do not have a full stomach.

What Shiatsu can do for you

As already stated, Shiatsu is a holistic treatment which aims to relieve dis-ease, revitalise the body and regenerate the innate self-curative powers available to us all.

By improving the balance of Ki, treatment by Shiatsu can relieve and heal many ailments such as:

Stress and tension
Menstrual problems
Backache
Headache
Aches and pains

Shiatsu can improve:
Nervous system
Digestion
Libido
Health during pregnancy
Posture
Stamina
Vitality
Body, mind and spirit.

In addition to the Shiatsu massage session, therapy can include moxibustion and cupping (see Chapter 'Traditional Chinese Medicine'), advice on lifestyle and diet, and instruction in 'Do-in' - a Japanese form of self-help treatment consisting of breathing, stretching, meditation and corrective exercises.

Where to find out more

Ridolfi, Ray, *Alternative Health, Shiatsu*, Optima, England, 1990.
Ohashi, Wataru, *Shaitsu Do It Yourself*, Unwin, London, 1979.
Namikoshi, Toru, *Shiatsu and Stretching*, Napan Publications, Japan, 1985.

The Motherpeace Round Tarot

The Motherpeace Round Tarot was originated by Karen Vogel in 1981, and was developed to show positive female images for this art of divination. By its development we are re-introduced and put in contact with the ancient goddesses of prehistoric times who can still impart their powers of wisdom and healing to us.

A brief history of matriarchal culture

Some 5,000 years ago peace-giving, life-loving goddesses were worshipped all around the globe from North America to the Mediterranean, across India and Eqypt. The Great Mother figure was honoured for her creative and spiritual power and images, statues and stone inscriptions still survive today to tell the story of her culture.

In Ireland, Brigit was goddess of fertility in pagan times. She was represented by a sun symbol, the Brigit's Cross. Not only was she the goddess of poets, she was also the protector of beasts and often her symbol can be seen cut in stone above the doors of cattle sheds. Brigit's Day was the first day of spring, 1 February, in pagan times. Brigit also represented fire and was the goddess of healing. In Scotland she was known as Brechin, in Switzerland as Brigantii, in Sanskrit as Brhaspti and in Old Norse as Bragi.

Medb was the ambiguous goddess of dawn and dusk, light and darkness. In Sanskrit her name was Madhu (meaning honey or sweet drink), in English it was Mead (now the name of a honey or sweet drink as well), and in India it was Madhu.

The triple goddess or moon goddess is every woman; the mother who brings man into the world, the nymph who lies with him and the old hag who buries him. After the advent of patriarchy the male still had to mate with the old hag (known in Gaelic as the cailleach) before claiming sovereignty. The triple goddess is queen of land, sea and air, of the conscious and unconscious, and of the soul.

Another acclaimed example of the important role woman played in prehistoric times is seen in the Síle na Gig, a group of female sculptures which survive to this day. The Síle na Gig are nude female figures, shown face on, with splayed legs displaying the female reproductive organs, the symbol of fertility. They are found especially in Ireland, as well as in Britain and France.

With the development of our patriarchal cultures this peaceful, matriarchal world was destroyed and the Great Mother religion was practised only in secret.

Images seen on the Motherpeace Tarot (which is illustrated by Vicki Noble) are largely taken from genuine archaeological artifacts predating Christianity and our patriarchal culture, which have been found in ancient sites all over the world.

The symbolism of the Motherpeace Tarot

Traditional Tarots are oblong, symbolising all that is fixed and inflexible, bearing messages which originate from a patriarchal culture. In contrast, the Motherpeace Tarot is circular which, since megalithic times, has been the sign of the infinity of creation and procreation. It is also the symbol of the moon, which in turn is the symbol of the mysterious, female aspect of things, of hidden power and the secrets of the sub-conscious. The moon is also acknowledged as a symbol of imagination, intuition and healing powers.

As in traditional Tarot decks, Motherpeace has 78 images in all: 22 Major Arcana and 56 Minor Arcana. The Major Arcana indicate cosmic principals and transformations of the human soul, while the Minor Arcana are of the human and elemental worlds.

In contrast to the Court Cards of the traditional tarot (the Page, the Knight, the Queen and the King), Motherpeace has four different images: the Daughter, the Son, the Priestess and the Shaman (spiritual tribal healer).

Motherpeace are very visual and brightly coloured. Each face has an expression; each individual is acting in some manner. Their surroundings include all manner of things in the universe from birds to animals, from fish to plants and flowers. Each and

38

every image has its own symbolism and only by meditating on it in peace and harmony with your surroundings will you be able to read the messages of the Motherpeace Round Tarot.

How to use Motherpeace Round Tarot

Whether reading the Motherpeace Round Tarot from a full spread or reading cards individually, remember to treat them with respect.

The designs and symbolism of these cards are like no other Tarot deck. When you first see them take time to look at each one and study them individually. Look at them and meditate, and allow yourself to enter the world of self-transformation. To gain the most from these cards you must drop any preconceived ideas you have and let the pictures speak for themselves.

Every face has its own individual expression, each chosen colour has its own meaning. The actions you see have a meaning of their own. Are they carefree, or heavy with sadness? The cards have illustrations of all the elements to be found in the universe: birds, beasts, fish, plants, flowers. Some are a joyous celebration, some hold a warning. When you read a card take time to understand its individual meaning from the symbols you are reading. Keep your mind at peace and enter a new world.

With Motherpeace Round Tarot the world of the patriarch is held at bay. You have the power to see the story unfold. What you read in it is up to you.

Some examples of the Motherpeace Round Tarot

Major Arcana - XX Judgement
A female symbol in purple stands atop the globe, casting the colours of the rainbow from her heart over the world.

This could be interpreted as an open-hearted love and compassion for others and for the self. One has transcended the old self and risen to a new consciousness.

Minor Arcana - 10 Discs
A figure brings new life into the world, supported by friends and surrounded by a circle of supporters.

Discs stand for things of the earth, the body, work, money. This card could mean that you are bringing a new project into being with the helpful support of the community.

Major Arcana - XVII Star

As gentle rain falls, a female bathes in a pool surrounded by lilies, rushes and flowers. The star shines down and a bird takes flight.

The rain represents grace descending on those open to receive it, the star stands for hope and freedom, and Ishtar the goddess of love. The act of cleansing represents a new openness and the ability for self-healing.

A simple reading

Shuffle the full deck, then place it face downwards on a flat surface. Now, cut the deck to the left into three sections. Whenever you cut a Tarot deck ensure you always make a left-hand cut. This is because the left part of your body is governed by the right-hand part of the brain, the side of creativity and intuition. Using the left hand also means that you are using the hand nearest the heart. Now, pick up the three sections so that the section that was originally on top is now on the bottom. Then, with a simple question in your mind and allowing your intuition to take control, turn over the card on top.

Study the card in your hand. Take time to accept and understand its symbolism. Allow yourself to surrender to the power of the visual image and reflect on it. Use your imagination and sub-conscious intuitive powers to receive the message. The card will speak to you and give you the answer to your question if you allow it.

A full spread

A full spread in Motherpeace requires the use of at least 11 cards. (The way to place the spread is illustrated in the booklet which accompanies the Motherpeace Tarot.)

To get an answer to the outcome of the spread you need a Major Arcana card. If the last card is not a Major Arcana then turn over another. If this is again a Minor Arcana try again. Do not turn over more than three at the end of the spread. If at the end of turning over three extra cards you are still without a

Major Arcana this means the answer is not clear at the present time. Read the Minor Arcana card which was originally placed at the end of the spread and put the others back into the deck.

This is a basic explanation of the Motherpeace Tarot. A reader has to see and feel the cards in order to understand their influence and guidance.

Where to find out more

Motherpeace Round Tarot, *Motherpeace: A Way to the Goddess through Myth, Art and Tarot*, Motherpeace Round Tarot, California, and US Games Systems Inc, 1981.

Hypnotherapy

How would you react if you were told that you have a friend who can help you attain personal achievements which seem impossible if you attempt them alone? That with this friend's help you can heal yourself of illness without need of medical prescriptions, stop smoking without suffering any withdrawal symptoms, undergo surgical and dental treatment without anaesthetic and without pain? That this ally will help you boost your performance, take away stress, improve your self-confidence, help you become more successful in your business and personal life? That with this friend on your side you can lose or gain weight, pass exams, cease or decrease alcohol consumption, look younger, feel fitter, and best of all achieve all these changes with little conscious effort on your part?

Does this sound like a dream? Well, it is a reality and the good news is that everyone has this friend within them. This ally which can make the seemingly impossible become reality is the sub-conscious, that invisible part of every one of us which affects our lives so deeply yet stays hidden beneath our surface conscious selves. To get this ally to work on our behalf is simple; for all it requires is a suggestion to be implanted in order for that wish to become a fact. Your sub-conscious self, the id, will work quietly and calmly on your conscious self, the ego, until the wish has become reality.

The philosophy behind hypnotherapy

Hypnotherapy - theraphy through hypnosis - brings wholeness to people through stimulating the mind. The one embryo from which we each originate divides into three; one develops the mind, one the skin, bones and organs, and the other the hormone glands. It is the mind which controls our hormones, and our physical and mental abilities. The mind is a source of enormous power and potential.

Most illnesses are psychosomatic (the *psyche* is the mind working on the *soma*, the body). The mind tells the body that there is disharmony between the two. In answer to this, our nervous system reacts with all sorts of complaints such as skin disorders, organ disfunctions and dependencies on alcohol or nicotine. Our nervous systems are made up of the voluntary and the autonomic, the latter being controlled by our sub-conscious. To return to harmony we must therefore contact our sub-conscious.

Hypnotherapy gives us access to the sub-conscious through the conscious mind. In order for it to work a person must be relaxed and at ease, and co-operate fully with the therapist. While in an altered state of attention, the practitioner talks to the sub-conscious mind and implants a suggestion which, if accepted by the conscious mind, will be passed into the sub-conscious and work as an ally on our behalf.

The analogy of the iceberg helps us to understand the difference between our sub-conscious and conscious selves. Only the very tip of the iceberg floats above the surface, visible to the world, yet beneath the surface of the water lies a huge block of ice which uses its power to forge the direction in which the entire iceberg will travel.

In the same way, we show to the world our conscious self, the tip of the iceberg. Yet we are powered by our sub-conscious. The sub-conscious is that part of us that stores away information from our earliest days and can affect our self-image and our future behaviour without even revealing that it exists.

A short history of hypnotherapy

There is evidence that a form of sleep-induced hypnotherapy was used for the treatment of illness by the Druids, the Incas, the Ancient Greeks and the Egyptians in the days before anaesthesia.

In more recent times, about 1780, an Austrian doctor, Mesmer, believed a similar induced state, which he accredited to animal magnetism, was capable of being brought about by those who were in touch with astral power. This was called mesmerism and was popular in the treatment of patients for a while on the Continent. Of course, over the following years, there was much controversy about its potential healing abilities especially as Mesmer was considered to be a poseur by some of his colleagues. Still, it seemed to work in some cases.

In the 1840s a British doctor, James Braid, proved with experimentation that mesmerism could be induced without any recourse to the stars. This helped it become more acceptable to the general public. Some time later, following the successful treatments of a Scottish doctor, James Esdail, the French Royal Academy of Sciences conducted an investigation which returned a favourable report on its use. However, the discovery of anaesthetics was made around the same time and the majority of the medical profession found this method more effective for use in painless surgery.

Meanwhile a French general practitioner, Dr Liebault of Nancy, had been quietly treating his patients for twenty years by using what is now known as hypnotherapy. His method used neither drugs nor mysticism, but only the induced relaxed state of hypnosis through which he would suggest to the person to follow his instructions and to expect specific healing results. Dr Liebault's treatments proved successful and when a renowned doctor called Bernheim discovered Liebault's methods, he began to study them for his own use. By the 1880s Bernheim was treating his own patients with hypnotherapy and it was beginning to be accepted by his colleagues.

Freud found it impossible to induce his patients into a hypnotic state and so rejected it. His immense power within the medical community and among his disciples meant that hypnotherapy did not reach its potential, despite the fact that the British Medical Association, after many investigations, confirmed its viability in 1892. Subsequently, in the late 1940s, the BMA finally established hypnotherapy as a recognised medical aid.

How hynotherapy works

In order to overcome dis-ease it is necessary that a person be at ease, especially with herself. Hypnotherapy works on the basis that when in an altered state of mind a person enjoys a greatly increased suggestibility. Through this the practitioner can suggest to the sub-conscious that, working with the help of our most powerful ally, our mind, we can free our innate energy and inner resources and so put into action our recuperative and healing powers.

Although *hypnos* is the Greek word for 'sleep', you will not be asleep, when undergoing a therapy session The practitioner will merely help you reach a state of deep relaxation in mind and body. You will be acutely aware of what is going on, and as any suggestion has to be filtered through the conscious mind, nothing alien to the sub-conscious will be accepted. This is why in order to be a successful patient in hypnotherapy you must first of all want to change on a conscious level before your sub-conscious can go to work on fulfilling that wish.

Hypnotherapy puts our sub-conscious mind to work, to effectively relieve pain and treat and cure functional disorders, as well as helping us to live healthier, happier lives in which we reach our true potential. It is not a miracle cure. The cure is within a person, and hypnotherapy enables the person to find that cure and get it to work. A patient therefore must co-operate with the hypnotherapist. An ideal patient is imaginative and intelligent and wishes to undergo such treatment to achieve her goal,

In some ways hypnotherapy is like the effect of a lullaby on a child at bedtime. This is the time when the child's mind is most relaxed and receptive. By consoling with words of love and security, repeated time and again, the parent rids the child's mind of fears. (In China mothers use this approach to relax their children at bedtime in order to overcome the problem of bed-wetting.)

The clinical hypnotherapist is well versed in psychology and physiology. She will first of all attempt to discover the cause of the problem, then suggest to the sub-conscious that the cause will be overcome. Through repetition of such suggestion it is possible for the symptom to be cured. In the treatment of a cigarette smoker, for example, the hypnotherapist will try to discover the cause of the addiction, before going on to help the person overcome the need for cigarettes.

In some cases, such as asthma patients or those suffering from phobias, a form of regression is used where the practitioner will carefully take the person back to an earlier age when the first attack occurred. When the reason for that first attack is found, the hypnotherapist can then suggest that the person is no

45

longer apprehensive and that the sub-conscious fear is capable of being dealt with. A suggestion is made that should another attack take place the person will be relaxed and confident, capable of dealing with it. In this way it allows the person to effect a self-cure.

Some of the benefits of hypnotherapy

One of the main benefits of this treatment is that it allows you to alleviate suffering, which has manifested itself in dis-ease in the mind or body, by gaining control over yourself through beneficial relaxation techniques. With hypnotherapy there are no damaging side-effects and no fears of over-dosing.

Hypnotheraphy is particularly effective in the treatment of skin diseases. Skin is the mirror of the mind. When the mind is in turmoil, when events are just too much to cope with, the mind will communicate these disharmonies to the skin and it may erupt in a rash, or in other ailments such as psoriasis or dermatitis. Skin ailments are caused by a disharmony in hormone production which is produced by the brain when it is muddled (hormone comes from the Greek for 'messenger'). If you find the reason for such confusion ie unresolved problems of one sort or another, and resolve them, then the brain, the hormones and the skin can be brought into harmony again.

Hypnotherapy is especially helpful in accident cases where the victim needs immediate surgery but cannot be given an anaesthetic because of a full stomach. In such cases the person might be offered hypnotherapy and a local anaesthetic before being operated on. This has proven very successful. It can also be used where the person cannot have a full anaesthetic because of bronchial complaints.

Hypnotherapy helps to lessen anxiety before an operation and to lessen the pain during and after it. If a person is tense the pain is intensified. If the person is relaxed the pain is relieved. If the person is totally relaxed the pain is abolished.

In childbirth, relaxation techniques enable women to enjoy the birth of their children without fear or pain. This is particularly successful when a pregnant woman learns the secret of relaxation right from the start so she has learnt how certain muscles relax and contract, to enable the baby's pathway to be unhindered as it makes its way into the world. These techniques can also help control morning-sickness.

What hypnotherapy can do for you

If an introvert was told she could broadcast successfully to the nation, if someone who suffered from aerophobia was assured she could soon enjoy flying the Atlantic ... On a conscious level this would not be accepted at all and the person would put up barriers in the sub-conscious to prohibit these things from happening.

However, under hypnotic suggestion the conscious self is dormant and so the suggestion is made to the sub-conscious. Once implanted in the sub-conscious, your friend and ally will steer a course, as does the base of that iceberg, mentioned earlier, to ensure that the goal is achieved.

Whatever dis-ease you are suffering from, whether it be physical, social, psychological or emotional, you can get that friend, your sub-conscious, to work for you to overcome it.

A session

Hypnotherapy works best when the person co-operates fully with the therapist. At the beginning of a session the therapist will spend a lot of time talking to you because it is important that you build up a rapport, that she finds out what makes you tick, what is important to you, what holds you back.

Hypnotherapy is all about relaxation and you will find a session very enjoyable. You will be seated in a comfortable chair, in a comfortable position, and when you are ready the therapist will talk to you gently and calmly, suggesting that you are relaxed in mind and body. Soon you will begin to feel relaxed and drowsy and will feel the need to close your eyes. However, you will be aware of everything that is going on around you while in this relaxed state. At no time will you lose control of your own mind. You can accept or reject any suggestion made. To relax you deeper the therapist might play some background music, then suggest that you are sitting on a sandy beach with the tide lapping on the shore and the sun making your skin warm, or that you are walking in a beautiful garden full of your favourite flowers and shrubs.

Because your mind is now in a happy, relaxed state, it is open to the suggestion that you are able to relax and cope with any event which might happen. It may be suggested that your inner powers of healing are now going to work inside your body; it may be that from this moment you are no longer a smoker; it may be that your powers of concentration have improved so much that you can now learn quickly and easily.

All the time you are acutely aware of what is going on, though your body will feel heavy and your eyes drowsy. The therapist will be alert as to your depth of relaxation and when you are brought back to your conscious state you will still feel relaxed and rested.

A session can last 1-2 hours, and the number of sessions required depends on the nature of the problem and on your personality. If you have accepted the suggestions made to your sub-conscious during the session you will soon find yourself reacting in a controlled manner to your particular problem. If it is asthma you will find you can control your breathing, while practising relaxation techniques; if it is a too-large appetite, you will find yourself rejecting that extra mouthful. The more you allow your sub-conscious to help you relax the more you will achieve. This is called self-hypnosis or auto-suggestion and can be used any time, anywhere, for overcoming any problem.

Self-hypnosis or auto-suggestion

Self-hypnosis, also known as auto-suggestion, is another form of hypnotherapy but one which can be practised when alone. It can help in all sorts of situations, to enhance performance, to improve concentration, to induce sleep, to instil confidence.

The mind is like a radio-receiver; it can broadcast positive or negative signals. We so easily accept without question crises, disappointments and failure. Why do we find it so difficult to accept instead joy, success and happiness? How often have you come across someone who declares 'I'm never ill', and never is, someone who says 'of course this project will succeed' and the project does. It's a self-fulfilling prophecy. If we expect failure, we will fail. In the same way if we expect to succeed then we will succeed. An infant succeeds in walking and talking because that infant has never been taught to fail.

It is just as easy to accept good thoughts as it is to accept bad thoughts. The way to do this is to re-train our sub-conscious to accept good, positive thoughts instead of immediately reacting to a situation in a negative manner, putting up barriers to decisive action.

To enter our sub-conscious we must have our guard relaxed, and so the secret is to learn to go into deep relaxation. A therapist can help you in this by implanting a post-hypnotic suggestion in your mind which will enable you relax in your own environment, and so with practice you can train your sub-conscious to react in a more favourable manner.

Self-hypnosis would be particularly helpful to an expectant mother who would need to be in control, in the event of starting her labour at a time or in a place far distant from her therapist. The same would apply to an asthma sufferer who would need to be able to control the attack when alone and often during 'unsociable' hours.

Fear of undergoing dental treatment can also be helped through relaxation exercises. Instead of dreading the visit and anticipating pain, take time to relax at home and, instead, anticipate peace and relaxation. Relax again during the visit itself and you will feel no pain.

Instead of tensing up when facing an interview or an important meeting, take time at home to relax deeply. Visualise the meeting going well and coming to an end with your confidence intact and your abilities shown up in a good light. Once you have implanted a successful outcome in your sub-conscious it will quietly work towards achieving that aim for you, guiding you to say the right things and to act in the right manner.

Whatever problem you need to resolve, remember that hypnotherapy is a simple process of using relaxation to help your true ally, your own mind, to achieve your goals.

Where to find out more

Oakley, Gilbert ,*The Power of Self-Hypnosis*, W Foulsham & Co, England, 1989.
Markham, Ursula ,*Alternative Health, Hypnosis*, Optima, England, 1989.
Gibson, Dr Jack, *The Life and Times of an Irish Hypnotherapist*, Mercier Press, Ireland, 1989.
Sheet, Roger, *Hypnotherapy, Is It For You?* Element Books, England, 1988.

Numerology

Do you have a lucky number? What made you choose it and how important is it to you? Would you feel unsafe living in a house numbered 13, or on floor 13 of an apartment block?

Why is the number 7 considered to be lucky? Why do Japanese parents first count the number of brush strokes required before choosing a suitable name for their child?

A brief background to numerology

There is proof that the symbolism of numbers has been an integral part of human living since the days of the cave people. It was the Greek philosopher and mathematician, Pythagoras, who originated the science of numbers in about the sixth century BC. Pythagoras believed that 'everything is number' and that therefore number is an essential part of our world. What number of protons, neutrons and electrons does it take to make an atom, for example? How many atoms make up a molecule? How many molecules make a petal? How many petals make a flower?

Our prehistoric ancestors used number to communicate long before any alphabet was developed. The study of numbers is also closely linked with astrology because everything in our world has a numerical base. There are 28 days to a lunar cycle, and each stage of its cycle takes 7 days. There are 12 months in the year and 12 signs of the horoscope in western astrology.

Numerology concerns only those numbers from 1 - 9, because every other number, together with 0, is a combination of these single digits. The study of numbers is the study of the symbols for numbers and their significance. Take, for example, the figure 2. It can stand for partnership, for co-operation, for, working in conjunction with another, for seeing two sides of an argument, for duplicity. The figure 5, for example, symbolises the 5 senses, the person who is sensual and sexual, but perhaps not

50

intellectual. A more detailed explanation of the symbolism of numbers follows.

The magic of numbers

Numerologists are consulted by all kinds of people for all kinds of reasons - to develop company names, brand names, stage names, pen names and their own names. Usually they wish to attain more advantageous sets of numbers; the American numerologist Stephen Calia changed the spelling of his first name from Steven to Stephen in order to fill in a number gap in his life.

Do you find you change your attitudes with a change of name? For instance, does the Margaret who is a member of the board of directors show a different personality to the Maggie who meets people for lunch after the board meeting? You may feel there is some balance missing in your life. If so, this could be due to the lack of Karmic numbers missing in your name; these numbers are important in rounding out a personality. If you are not living in harmony with yourself, or with others, a subtle change in your name may make all the difference.

Numbers and you

Everyone is made up of numbers. You have two eyes, two ears, one nose, one mouth. You also have numbers which help make up your personality and your attitude to life. What makes us look, feel, and act differently to others can be partly determined by the different numbers which make up each of us.

Your most important numbers are
Your **birth number** - based on your date of birth
Your **name number** - based on the sum of the letters of your name
Your **ego number** - or conscious self - based on the sum of the vowels in your name
Your **id number** or unconscious self - based on the sum of the consonants in your name

Calculations can be further based on the number of the house where you live, your phone number, and any other numbers that are part of your life. Naturally you can then study whether your numbers are in harmony with your partner, family members, with colleagues and rivals, and with the planetary cycle and the solar cycle.

Although numerology is a science, there is no need to be put off by scientific terminology; at its most basic level numerology is simple to study. All you need is a pencil and pad, and the ability to add.

Discovering your numbers

Your birth number
To discover the influence of numbers in your life, you must first work out your birth number. This is your most important number because it is based on the day you were born, and is therefore influenced by the positions of the planets and the moon and the sun at that time. Unlike your name number, your birth number cannot be changed at will and you will always be affected by the positive and negative attributes of this number. It is also known as your destiny number or your lucky number.

To discover your birth number, you first of all write out your date of birth as in the following example. The example is for Marianne Neil born on 15 February, 1988

15 + 2 + 1988.

Now add each digit separately to the next digit, eg:
1 + 5 = 6, + 2 = 8, + 1 = 9, + 9 = 18, + 8 = 26, + 8 = 34

As we are looking for a single digit we now add 3 + 4 = 7
The birth number, therefore, is 7.

Your name number
Numerology was originally based on the numeric values taken from the Hebraic alphabet which had only 21 letters and no vowels. The numbers for the 5 vowels we use are taken from the Greek alphabet, A for Alpha = 1, E for Epsilon = 5, etc. The following table shows the numeric values for each of the 26 letters of our alphabet:

1	2	3	4	5	6	7	8	9
A	B	C	D	E	F	G	H	I
J	K	L	M	N	O	P	Q	R
S	T	U	V	W	X	Y	Z	

It is important to note at this point that if you are to discover your ego number (conscious self) and id number (Unconscious Self) you must count the numbers for the vowels and the consonants separately. To save time, this can be done when calculating the name number, as set out in our example, Marianne Neil. Again we are looking for single digits, so the total must be added together until a single digit is found.

Id Number :		4	9	5 5		5		3	= 31 = 4
	M A	R I	A N	N E		N E	I	L	
Ego Number :		1	9 1		5		5 9		= 30 = 3

Now add the two numbers together for the name number: = 7

Accord numbers
The following is a Table of Accord, which shows if your name number is in accord with your birth number

Birth Number	Name Positive	Numbers Neutral	Negative
1	1, 2, 3, 9	4 8	5, 6, 7
2	2, 3, 4	1, 5, 9	6, 7, 8
3	3, 4, 5	2, 6	1, 7, 8, 9
4	4, 5, 6	3, 7	1, 2, 8, 9
5	5, 6, 7	4, 8	1, 2, 3, 9
6	6, 7, 8	1, 5, 9	2, 3, 4
7	1, 7, 8, 9	2, 6	3, 4, 5
8	1, 2, 8, 9	3, 7	4, 5, 6
9	1, 2, 3, 9	4, 8	5, 6, 7

Marianne Neil's birth number of 7 is in accord with her name number of 7. She would be well advised not to change the spelling of her first name to Mary Anne this would give her a name number of 5, which would be incompatible with her birth number of 7. She could, however, change the spelling to Marion

Neil, to have a name number of 1 which is in accord with her birth number of 7.

Ego and Id numbers
In order to be happy with yourself and the world, your ego and your Id numbers must be in harmony. If they are not, there is sure to be inner strife resulting in tensions between your hidden self and your open self.

The vowel numbers (ego) and the consonant numbers (Id) must agree, that is, both must be even, or both odd. In Marianne Neil's case we can see that her ego number is 3 and her Id 4. They are therefore in disharmony. In her case a simple addition to her name can bring about harmony between her ego and her Id, without having an adverse effect on the harmony between her birth number and her name number. All she has to do is add the letter 'L' to her surname, and this is the result:

Id Number		4	9		5	5		5		3	3	≈ 34 ≈ 7
	M A R I A N N E				N E I L L							
Ego Number			1	9	1		5		5	9		≈ 30 ≈ 3

This now gives her a new name number of: 10 = 1.

Look back at the Table of Accord, and you will see that her birth number of 7 is in accord with her new name number of 1

What the numbers mean

Now that you have discovered your own birth, name, ego and Id numbers, check the following guide to see how your numbers have influenced your life. This guide is made up of keywords, but there is much more to numerology than can be outlined here. To find out more look out for the books mentioned at the end of this chapter.

The number 1
1 as a birth number
Symbol of the rising sun, 1 stands for singularity, for being first, for new beginnings, for innovation, for leading, for ambition, for

single-mindedness, for sexual awakening and adventure. 1 also stands for childishness, isolation and self absorption.

1 as a name number
No. 1's adore the sun, the outdoors, scrambling about forests and scaling mountains. 1's like to give advice and be of help to others.

1 as an ego number
1's are open, friendly and confident, make good leaders and take responsibility. However, they also tend to believe themselves superior and don't like to dirty their hands doing manual work.

1 as an Id number
1's believe in their own self-worth and are driven to put the world to rights. With high standards they don't have much patience for weaker people. Their ability to see sun behind clouds speeds recovery from setbacks and never allows for self-pity.

The number 2
2 as a birth number
The symbol of the Moon, 2's are introverted and thoughtful, sensitive and intuitive. With an ability to see both sides of an argument, 2's will be a boon to any partnership and will work best with others. 2 also stands for duplicity, self-consciousness and reclusivity.

2 as a name number
2's are night owls and can be unsettled by the phases of the Moon. 2's enjoy the elements, living close to the sea or a river and the company of positive people.

2 as an ego number
2's enjoy learning and prefer being a follower than a leader. Being rather shy, people may find you difficult to get to know. 2's are influenced by other people's opinion and their environment, and need a warm, loving relationship in order to blossom.

2 as an Id number
2's have an imaginative inner life and are often psychic. Reading

and artistic pursuits interest 2's who enjoy their own company. Mood swings can change from self-sufficiency to depression.

The number 3
3 as a birth number
3 symbolises intelligence, wisdom, imagination and dynamism. While being sociable and convivial, they also like to learn and are rather spiritual. 3's like to spend money and gamble, and as they don't like being alone should choose their friends and partners carefully.

3 as a name number
Being dynamic 3's love the open road and take to it in fast cars, on foot or by bike, but preferably not too early in the morning. An extrovert, sometimes 3 can go over the top a little.

3 as an ego number
Extrovert, friendly and confident. When something rattles that confidence. 3's may tend to turn to drink or drugs to alleviate uncertainties. Easily bored, 3's need to be stimulated and challenged in their job and their home.

3 as an Id number
Religion is important to 3's, but their strong sexual urge, causing temptation, can lead to repression and guilt. 3's are strongly intuitive and often have prophetic insights and dreams.

The number 4
4 as a birth number
4 represents stability and dedication. 4 makes a a good friend and is honest and law abiding. Stability is important because underneath an air of reticence and calm 4's suffer from periods of self doubt resulting in anxiety.

4 as a name number
4's won't win any fashion show, but will win hearts with large shows of generosity, while being rather miserly with smaller sums. Enjoying nature and down to earth creativity, 4's also have an interest in the occult.

4 as an ego number
With an outward air of stability and dependability, 4's long for

variety in their lives, so do well working independently with plenty of changes of scenery. 4's are friendly but need to maintain their freedom.

4 as an Id number

Full of creativity and intuition, 4's are bursting with great ideas and their stubbornness and persistence can help them see an idea through. While needing a pleasant environment, 4's also like to keep on the move, because they are fearful of entrapment.

The number 5
5 as a birth number

The symbol of Mercury, 5's are intelligent and quick. They excel at communication. Always on the move, 5's also enjoy reading, talking and entertaining others, but can show a quick temper due to a natural anxiety and impatience.

5 as a name number

5's are adventurers. They might not go further than their own gardens, but will be at their best meeting people and investigating their backgrounds, surrounded by good music and drama, and good food.

5 as an ego number

Quick thinkers, 5's are also quick learners and assimilate information rapidly. Enjoying a challenge 5's will happily try to solve any problem, whether they are qualified or not, but they don't suffer fools gladly.

5 as an Id number

Always interested in a challenge, 5's love travelling, learning and adventure. This can often make them feel restless and dissatisfied with their present lifestyle if they don't have the ability to take off at a moment's notice. 5's should trust their intuition and beware of 'get rich quick' schemes.

The number 6
6 as a birth number

Pleasant and friendly, helpful and artistic, 6 has lots of friends but also likes being alone. The home, relationships and family are important to 6, though selfishness and stubbornness can cause problems in communication.

6 as a name number
6's enjoy the great outdoors, especially in summer, as well as reading, singing and looking attractive to the eye with good clothes and jewellery. Just as well that 6's also enjoy searching for bargains!

6 as an ego number
Possibly the most balanced of all the ego numbers, 6's are a good mix of diffidence and extroversion. They enjoy bright, tasteful surroundings, and balance is important. While supporting law and order, 6's can see both sides of a problem which means they can sometimes be accused of sitting on the fence.

6 as an Id number
This is the number of harmony and peace, and a stable home and relationships are important to 6's. Interested in mysticism and philosophy, 6's have an eye for colour, line and form, and are creative.

The number 7
7 as a birth number
This is the number for spirituality and intrigue. 7's are cerebral, with a great liking for others and an intuitive understanding of them. Always interested in improving the mind, 7's tend to overlook improving their own appearance.

7 as a name number
While 7's don't like climbing mountains, they do like sitting beside the ocean or a friendly stream, especially if it is situated near a churchyard or cathedral. Enjoying mystery, 7's have a liking for history and archaeology.

7 as an ego number
While being very creative in the arts, 7's tend to lack direction and need support and encouragement, especially as they also lack staying power. Warm and sociable, 7's are popular but can be just as happy when alone, letting intuition guide them.

7 as an Id number
7's are often interested in the occult and have an instinctive knowledge which could make them good mediums or psychics.

Day dreamers, 7's are happy alone or in company, where they listen sympathetically to others and offer good advice.

The number 8
8 as a birth number
Responsible and self-controlled, 8's make good leaders because they mature early and have a realistic understanding of life. A little conservative, authority is important to 8's whose main fault lies in a lack of a sense of humour.

8 as a name number
8's usually love anything to do with the soil, including root vegetables. They also enjoy being in woods and mountains, near lakes and rivers; they like the company and wisdom of old people, and are in their element in winter.

8 as an ego number
Stability and conventionality are the keywords for this number. 8's plod along uncomplaining for years and don't like to be faced with sudden changes, except when it comes to their sex drive when they move very fast to fulfil this urge.

8 as an Id number
Loyal and dutiful, prudent and careful, 8's tend to keep their feelings to themselves and to put a brake on their ambitions, except where their sex urge takes over resulting in great drive and energy.

The number 9
9 as a birth number
Impatient and rash, fearless and strong, 9's are outgoing, confident and like to have their own way. They are idealists who are happy to lead but don't always see it through. Always open to new ideas, 9's like change and excitement, and often rush in without adequate preparation.

9 as a name number
9's like the best of both worlds, the quality of country life, the fast movement of the city. Enjoying colour and activity, 9's are often fond of sports and always enjoy a good laugh.

9 as an ego number

Although 9's like bright colours, issues tend to be in black and white, with no in-between. Frankness can lead to arguments with friends and family, but a 9's generosity and enthusiasm will quickly mend any fissures.

9 as an Id number

A 9 Id means inner turbulence, and an obsession to strive to do better. 9's should listen to their inner hunches for guidance when looking for a career. Sex is important to a 9, though constancy is not, because they hate to be enclosed in a room or a relationship.

Where to find out more

Buess, Lynn M, *Numerology for the New Age*, Devors, California, USA, 1978.
Fenton, Sasah (Ed), *The Aquarian Book of Fortune Telling*, Aquarian Press, England, 1987.
Stein, A, *Your Child's Numerology*, Future Publications, England, 1987.

Traditional Chinese Medicine
(TCM)

To the Chinese all things are made up of basic energy (known as Tao), which is manifest through the dynamic energy forces of Yin and Yang. Yin (female, negative) and Yang (male, positive) interact with one another and although they are opposites one cannot exist in isolation from the other. The balance between Yin and Yang is the energy balance known as Ch'i. In Chinese medical philosophy health is a state of energy balance within the body and this energy balance (Ch'i) is the primary element of all physiological activities.

Ch'i

Ch'i is a living force of Yin and Yang which circulates through the body in a defined cycle from point to point, from organ to organ. Ch'i channels (or meridians) cannot be seen in fact, but can be more easily understood if one imagines it moving in its defined cycle in much the same way as blood circulates through blood vessels around the body. Everyone is given a certain amount of Ch'i at birth and this level is reduced over the years with the 'wear and tear' of life. However, it is boosted when we take in food and oxygen.

The correct balance of Yin and Yang is responsible for harmony in the universe and in people. When the Ch'i is unbalanced, ill health results. When there is no Ch'i remaining, death occurs.

Yin and Yang

Yin symbolises the female, the earth, the moon, all that is

negative, cold, dark, passive and hidden.

Yang symbolises the male, the sky, the sun, all that is heat, light, active, readily apparent. As you can see from the symbol for Yin - Yang, each complements the other and neither is without the influence of the other.

Chinese medical philosophy

This philosophy of interaction follows through in Traditional Chinese Medicine (TCM). Organs are recognised in terms of their function and therefore their influence over other parts of the body. To the TCM practitioner a physiological organ such as the heart includes more than its structure and location. It also includes the overall effect the heart has on the rest of the body: the way the heart pumps affect the blood vessels, which in turn affect the blood circulation, which, again, affect the blood tissue. Taking another physiological organ such as the lungs; these affect the respiratory system which in turn affects the body and the skin. Therefore, when ill health occurs the TCM practitioner will work to either stimulate or sedate the levels of energy of designated areas of the body. The philosophy of TCM is to use drugs sparingly and keep the person fully conscious even under major surgery. This ensures that recovery is more rapid, natural and comfortable.

TCM treatment is holistic. Health is a balance between the body, the mind and the spirit. There are many differing treatments available under the term Traditional Chinese Medicine. If this philosophy appeals to you, you will want to find out more about acupuncture (or sedating, stimulating energy levels through the use of fine needles), moxibustion (stimulating or sedating energy levels with the help of moxa cones made from wormwood shrub), massage (by finger hand

and joint pressure) and shiatsu (by finger pressure; see separate chapter, 'Shiatsu'.)

A short history of acupuncture

Acupuncture is the best known of TCM treatments. Its origin is not certain, but it is believed to have been developed over the centuries from folk lore. It had been noticed that there was an increase in sensitivity of certain points of the body when an organ or its function was impaired and so the relationship between organ and illness was established. These areas of sensitivity are known as pathways for energy, or meridians. The Chinese believe that Ch'i circulates through the body in a defined cycle from meridian to meridian. By connecting with Ch'i through the correct meridian ill health can be treated This is the practice of acupuncture.

The earliest known text setting out the essential philosophy of acupuncture goes all the way back to Huang Ti (the Yellow Emperor), who lived around 2,500 BC. Historians have found needles made of iron, sharpened stone, bamboo splints or gold and silver, the latter being for the use of the very rich only. Nowadays some people use gold needles for stimulating Ch'i and silver needles for sedating Ch'i. Acupuncture has been used not only by the Chinese but right across the globe, for centuries. The Egyptians used it up to 3,000 years ago and Sri Lanka has evidence of its practice going back 1,000 years. Eskimos still use sharpened stones on specified points of their bodies to allay their ill health, the Bantu tribe of Africa scratch areas of their skin, a Brazilian tribe blow darts to certain points and the Arabs cauterise points in their ears.

Known as Bian during the Yin dynasty, the word acupuncture is derived from Latin, 'acus', meaning needle, and 'pungere' to pierce or puncture. It came to the West via Jesuit missionaries sent to Peking in the seventeenth century and is now becoming more and more popular to Westerners as a form of medical treatment.

How acupuncture works

Stated simply, acupuncture is a therapy which consists of the stimulation or sedation of Ch'i, the energy balance, through the use of very fine needles inserted into designated points of the skin It can also include the application of heat, and/or massage, or all three as a form of treatment.

These fine needles, now usually made from stainless steel, are placed in acupuncture points (also known as acupoints or acupores) whose precise locations are dependent on diagnosis undertaken by the practitioner. The points are chosen to connect to the energy pathways or meridians which in turn connect to the organ which is disfunctioning. The Chinese word for meridian is Ch'ing.

There are several different types of meridians within our bodies and all meridians start or end at our hands or feet.

The main meridians
There are 12 pairs of main meridians which give 24 direct pathways to each different organ. These main meridians have their pathways near the surface of the skin.

The extra meridians
There are 8 extra meridians which act as reservoirs for the main meridians.

'Lo' meridians
These are connecting meridians which join each main meridian to its paired Meridian.

Muscle meridians
These feed muscles and joints.

Divergent meridians
These diverge from the main meridians and carry energy to fight off harmful influences affecting organs.

The philosophy behind TCM is that microcosm affects macrocosm, in other words, 'that which is below is similar to that on high'. The Chinese believe that the five basic elements, fire, water, earth, metal and wood interact in a creative cycle to form all other substances. In TCM each of these elements is identified with a body organ. In this way the concord between each element and organ is used in diagnosis and treatment.

The following diagrams illustrate this philosophy, starting with the Cycle of Creation:

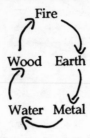

Here we see that:

>Fire generates Earth
>Earth generates Metal
>Metal obtains Water
>Water produces Wood
>Wood becomes Fire

Now look at the Cycle of Destruction:

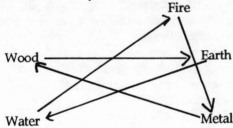

Here we see that

>Fire destroys Metal
>Earth absorbs Water
>Metal cuts down Wood
>Wood covers Earth
>Water puts out Fire

There is also a Cycle of Neutrality:

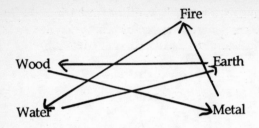

This cycle shows that:

Water does not affect Earth
Earth does not affect Wood
Wood does not affect Metal
Metal does not affect Fire
Fire does not affect Water

To each element, and therefore to each organ, one Yin and one Yang is assigned. Just as Ch'i is specific to TCM, so are two other organs: the heart constrictor, also known as the controller of the heart, which regulates and circulates energy, and the triple heater which protects and transports metabolic activity, and is also known as the three matabolisms.

Fire Yin - heart, heart constrictor (controller of the heart)
Yang - small intestine, triple heater (3 metabolisms)
Earth Yin - spleen, pancreas
Yang - stomach
Metal Yin - lungs
Yang - large intestine
Water Yin - kidneys
Yang - bladder
Wood Yin - liver
Yang - gall bladder

As stated before, when there is an imbalance of Ch'i within these organs, dis-ease and disharmony occur. Putting the elements and the organs together with their Yin and Yang balance, the practitioner then recognises that:

Wood (liver and gall bladder) fuels Fire (heart/heart constrictor, small intestine and triple heater).

Fire (heart/heart constrictor, small intestine and triple heater) generates Earth (spleen, pancreas and stomach).

Earth (spleen, pancreas and stomach) produces Metal (lungs and large intestine).

Metal (lungs, large intestine) holds Water (kidneys and bladder).

Water (kidney and bladder) nourishes Wood (liver and gall bladder).

An acupuncture session

You will discover that an initial session will include a diagnosis of the tongue and also the pulse and will last from 30-60 minutes. Acupuncture recognises twelve pulses in all, six on each wrist, each associated with a vital organ.

Remember disharmony means dis-ease so tell your practitioner of any problems you are encountering in your life, be they physical, spiritual or emotional, and this will help in the diagnosis for treatment.

The amount of treatments involved will depend on different factors relating to the symptom including your own recovery rate, the length of time you have been suffering from your illness, and its seriousness.

Advice on attending an acupuncturist

Go only to a recognised acupuncturist/TCM practitioner. Check if the practitioner belong to the Professional Register of Traditional Chinese Medicine. These practitioners are bound by a code of practice which includes the requirement to provide sterile procedures in their surgeries. Acupuncture needles are used on only one individual and are pre-sterilised by autoclave methods for safety.

TCM treatments are compatible with Western medicine, but make sure you inform the practitioner of any medicaments you are being prescribed.

Because of the way acupuncture is carried out, when attending a session be sure you do not wear tight clothing, jewellery, perfume, deodorant or heavy make-up.

What acupuncture can do for you

Acupuncture has no side effects or disagreeable after effects and gives immediate relief of pain. In some cases pain can cease immediately and often permanently. Some organs have a better response than others. For instance research shows that the liver responds best, followed by muscles, heart and bladder. Then kidney. Problems with the sense organs such as the ears and eyes can be improved, and acupuncture can actually increase muscular strength by improving the blood circulation and haemoglobin production which in turn improves muscle tissue.

Acupuncture alone can cure or relieve most ailments and TCM practitioners are confident that with their skill they can tailor a treatment to suit every person who is suffering from ill health due to infection, pain, addiction, or general dis-ease.

By stimulating resistance to disease, acupuncture enhances the body's natural powers of immunity. If you cannot bear the idea of needles being used in treatment, there are other avenues open to you as listed below. A practitioner will treat not only the physical but also the spiritual and psychological disorder. The following is just a sample of the divergent complaints which are successfully treated:

Angina and stroke
Bulimia and anorexia
Childbirth problems and miscarriage
Drug addictions
Lumbago rheumatism arthritis
Female and male infertility
PMS and menopausal problems
Nervous disorders
Mental disorders
Ulcers and stomach complaints

Other forms of acupuncture

For those who would not wish to be treated with the fine needles there are other forms of acupuncture available.

Laser: A laser beam works on only one wavelength so does not spread like ordinary light. Therefore the beam can be directed to the acupoint required without affecting any other part of the body. Weak lasers are used in acupuncture.

Sound: Sound and ultrasound absorbs energy and this energy can be changed to work in the required way on the body.

Other forms of TCM treatment

A TCM practitioner looks on treatment as holistic therapy, and will take into consideration the state of the body, the spirit and the emotions. The therapy chosen to cure your particular ailment might include a mix of acupuncture, massage, moxibustion, vacuuming, herbs, exercise, diet and general advice. Whichever treatment is used the basic philosophy remains the same, that illness or dis-ease is caused by an imbalance of Ch'i, the mix of Yin and Yang energy in your body.

Do it yourself acupuncture

It is possible to treat your own body by a form of acupuncture, without the use of needles but this is only advised if you have first had your dis-ease diagnosed by a practitioner, or in an emergency.

The advantages of DIY acupuncture is that you can follow up on sessions you have received with a practitioner in your own home, in your own time, and as often as you wish.

The acupuncture sites are from a quarter inch to three inches beneath the skin, and it is important to find the right site (See below for a publication on this.) The Chinese developed a measure which takes into account the different sizes of people, and this measure is called a Tsun. To find your Tsun measurement, just stretch out your middle finger, then bend it. The length of the outer part of the middle joint is the Tsun measurement which is proportional for your body.

When applying pressure to an acupoint, keep your finger (or

your knuckle) in place using the required pressure, and slowly rotate it over the acupoint. You will find the acupoint area is more tender than that of the surrounding area, and when pressure is applied correctly a tingling sensation will be felt. This is a sign that stimulation is occurring. If it hurts, use less pressure.

DIY acupuncture is often carried out by athletes before and after taking part in activity in order to perform for longer periods and to rehabilitate muscles under stress.

The following are examples of DIY acupuncture, but as mentioned earlier, if you are suffering ill health do first of all go to a practitioner and get a proper diagnosis.

Acupuncture and obesity

There are several acupoints you can use to treat obesity. The acupoint should be pressed deeply for several minutes when you feel hungry. The following are two examples of the areas to treat, and you should use the one which you feel suits you best.

The first place is on the abdomen acupoint which overlies the stomach. To find this, place fingers of left hand together and straight, then line up the tip of the index finger by the umbilicus. Now carefully open the gap between the little finger and the ring finger and just below the web is the acupoint you seek.

The second place can be found on either leg in the soft tissue on the outside of the shin. As an example, place your closed left hand sideways across your left leg just below the kneecap. Use the index finger of your right hand and place this just below the little finger of your left hand. To find the exact point the tip of your index finger on your left hand should be in line with the top joint of your little finger.

Acupuncture and menstrual problems

For menstrual difficulties there are several acupoints which can be used. For those suffering from PMT, use the ankle foot point. First of all find the rounded ankle bone on the inside of your left (or right) leg. Now place your four fingers together above it. The acupoint is just above your hand directly in line with the ankle bone. Apply pressure here for several days before your cycle and continue for several days after. For those suffering from heavy flow, place first two fingers together and put just below the umbilicus so that the tips of the fingers are in line with it. The acupoint is now just below these two fingers. Apply pressure here on the first day of your cycle and continue until it stops.

Acupressure and massage

Acupressure uses the same acupoints as those for acupuncture, but instead of needles uses fingertips. It is sometimes called acupuncture without needles, and can be used as a complement to acupuncture. The fingers massage in a clockwise direction to sedate and an anti-clockwise direction to stimulate.

In Western massage the practitioner massages to increase blood circulation around the body. In TCM, massage is used to stimulate points or entire meridians. Remedial massage is massage by the hands on certain areas of the body in order to produce the required effect on the corresponding organ or its function. There are two different ways to massage: An-mo which tones by pressing and rubbing, and Tui-Na which soothes and sedates by thrusting and rolling.

Massage is carried out not only by digital pressure but also by elbow pressure, stamping and scratching.

Moxibustion

Moxibustion is the burning of a moxa cone made from the wormwood plant (Artemisia vulgaris) on acupoints in order to stimulate or sedate the flow of Ch'i. It is used to supplement, or as a substitute for needle therapy. Moxibustion lasts from 3 - 20 minutes depending on the treatment.

There are three different sizes of moxa cones which can be used. The large cones, which are as big as a cherry, are used for stimulating energy and are removed when the person begins to feel discomfort from the heat. The smaller cones, which are the size of rice grains, are left on the skin to burn all the way down. This form of treatment can be painful and causes small blisters form on the skin. The smallest cones, the size of a pen point, are used in their hundreds in special situations. This form of treatment is more popular in Japan.

This form of treatment can be painful and causes small blisters form on the skin. The smallest cones, the size of a pen point, are used in their hundreds in special situations. This form of treatment is more popular in Japan.

The Chinese themselves prefer to use a moxa stick, which is similar to a lit cigarette and is held close to the acupoint until the person feels discomfort from the heat.

Moxibustion is practised using an electric moxa, which is held close to the skin. This does not leave any scarring.

Moxibustion can also be applied by placing the cone on top of an acupuncture needle and lighting it. The heat from the cone then passes down into the acupoint. This is a good treatment for pain relief and ease in muscular pain. Moxibustion should only be applied by a skilled practitioner.

Cupping

In cupping, a practitioner uses a jar or tube made of glass or bamboo to improve the flow of Ch'i. The jar is warmed, and this creates a vacuum inside. The warmed jar then attaches itself by suction to the required area of the skin and it clings to this position. The jar is left in this position for 10-15 minutes.

Cupping is a recognised treatment for arthritis and sprains, and is often used as a treatment for bronchial complaints, when medicinal herbs are first placed in the warmed jar so that their goodness is passed into the skin.

Cupping is also known as vacuuming.

Where to find out more

Nightengale, Dr Michael, *Alternative Health Acupuncture*, Optima, England, 1987.
Manaka, Yoshio (MD), and Ian A Urquart (Ph D), *A Layman's Guide to Acupuncture*, Weatherhill, New York and Japan, 1975.
McDonald, Alexander, *Acupuncture from Ancient Art to Modern Medicine*, Unwin Paperbacks, England, 1984.
Kenyon, Keith, (MD), Pressure Pints, *DIY Acupuncture Without Needles*, Arco Publishing Co. New York, 1985.

Homeopathy

Conventional medicine is called allopathy, and it is based on the philosophy of treating the dis-ease by attacking it with its opposite. Allopathy treats the disease itself, not its cause. When you are suffering from an illness a doctor practising allopathy will tend to prescribe a treatment from pharmaceutical medicine. Whether or not you are warned of the risk of side-effects, you may experience them by taking this treatment because, while the medicine attacks the specific illness, it may also have a detrimental effect on other parts of the body which are perfectly healthy.

Homeopathy, however, treats the whole person rather than just the dis-ease and has no side-effects. As it is given in microdoses there is no fear of taking an overdose.

The philosophy behind homeopathy

When we suffer any dis-ease we should listen to our body and hear what it is trying to tell us. The Greek 'father of medicine' Hippocrates taught, 'Let like be treated by like', and believed that both the physical and the psychological condition of the person should be taken into account if the correct remedy is to be found.

This same philosophy lies behind homeopathy, where the practitioner treats like with like, and it is the person who is treated, not the dis-ease. With homeopathy both the person's personality and the dis-ease are taken into account before a diagnosis is made. The remedy given will then help the person regain the natural balance which in turn will mean the regaining of good health. For this reason there is no 'overnight cure' using homeopathic remedies, but the person is put on a gradual road to recovery.

Homeopathy uses natural cures in microdoses. It has been

proven that the weaker the solution, the higher the potency. So it is a very safe form of treatment because there can be no overdosing. It is also ideal for chronic illness as there are no side-effects.

A short history of homeopathy

Christian Samuel Hahnemann was an allopathic doctor born in 1755 in Meissen, Germany. Though running a successful practice in allopathic medicine he became convinced that there must be some other form of treatment that would be more beneficial to the people he treated. Then a life-threatening illness of his daughter forced him to take steps to find a safer treatment.

At that time certain dis-eases were being treated by herbal remedies, such as using the South American bark Cinchona which provided quinine to treat malaria. Following Hippocrates' dictum, 'treat like with like', Hahnemann wanted to discover what would happen should a healthy person be treated with quinine. In good health, he took some cinchona himself and began to suffer the effects of malaria, symptoms such as high fever, sweating etc. This led him to believe that, 'It is only by the power of drugs to make you sick that they can cure sickness,' which agreed with a theory by Sydenham that the ague should be regarded as the body's way of fighting malaria, not malaria's way of fighting the body.

Hahnemann believed that to find out how a remedy could cure, it would first have to be 'proved' on a healthy person. Thus, the resulting dis-ease which developed in that person would show the dis-ease that the remedy would cure. He and others who followed after him personally 'proved' hundreds of homeopathic remedies to cure dis-eases.

Hahnemann's remedies were 'simples': single, uncompounded substances taken from herbs, minerals and snake venom. They required no compounding by the chemists and it was found that the more they were diluted the more potency they held. This meant that millions of remedies could be made from one drop of a particular extract from plant or mineral.

It wasn't long before homeopathy was seen as a great threat by general practitioners and chemists, who made their living by compounding drugs, and as their fears multiplied, homeopathy was banned by law in some countries. Hahnemann himself spent most of his latter years being persecuted for his beliefs and had to move from town to town, country to country. However, in 1836 a cholera epidemic raged through Vienna with 66 per cent of its victims dying. When homeopathy was used this cut the death rate to 30 per cent and so it became a more acceptable treatment. In Britain Frederick Quin became the first homeopathic doctor and he successfully treated the British royal family. Over the years their patronage has endured and this has enabled the establishment of several homeopathic hospitals in Britain.

Later, when medicine was nationalised in Britain in 1948, homeopathic treatment was included.

In recent years homeopathy has become more accepted by conventional medicine. General practitioners are now learning homeopathy after undergoing their full medical training and often treat persons with homeopathic remedies.

Animals, as well as people, can be successfully treated by these remedies. Before the advent of fertilizers and weedkillers, animals would naturally find their own remedy in the herbs they ate. Now those natural remedies are disappearing, but some animals are treated by homeopathic vets who again take into consideration the personality of the animal together with its complaint. One example of its success is in the prevention of mastitis. When a dairy cow suffers from mastitis she is usually treated with an antibiotic; this in turn affects the milk yield which has to be thrown away, resulting in a financial loss to the farmer. With a homeopathic remedy, however, mastitis is by and large prevented and when it does occur there is no side effect on the milk yield.

How homeopathy works

The reasoning behind homeopathy is to create a cure from a fractional dose of something which, in a larger dose, would create an illness. Homeopathic remedies are taken from extracts of plants, minerals or snake venom. There is no chemical process involved. A drop of this extract is merely diluted in 100 drops of water or alcohol/water mix. This dilution is then seccused (shaken vigorously) which makes it more potent. This potency (or stage) is then diluted with another 100 drops of water or alcohol/water mix and seccused, so at the third stage the remedy is 1,000,000 times diluted. A drop or two of the final potency is then added to a bottle of sugar pills and this is the 'remedy' prescribed.

No one yet fully understands how a solution which is diluted so many times could possibly contain a cure. A fundamental law of homeopathy, however, is taken from the studies of physicists Ardnt and Schultz who discovered that:

> Weak strength stimuli encourages life activity
> Medium strength stimuli impedes life activity
> Strong strength stimuli destroys life activity

Allopathic doctors often accuse homeopathic practitioners of treating persons with a 'placebo' (medicine given to humour, rather than to cure), yet as shown above animals are successfully treated with homeopathic remedies and no one could persuade them of believing in the need for a placebo.

Some say water changes in form (ie a snowflake is a different form of a water particle) and so, as the water changes form with each dilution and seccusion it enables the potency to change too. No one asks a bee how it can fly when its design is, apparently, in contradiction to aerodynamics. Yet a bee can and does fly. And so homeopathy works, whether or not it follows the rules set down by science.

What homeopathy can do for you

The Greek medical researcher Paracelsus said, 'All things are poison, for there is nothing without poisonous qualities. It is only the dose which makes a thing a poison.' This is allowed in conventional medical practice with the use of innoculations and vaccinations which work in fighting off dis-eases such as TB, polio and rubella. And government agencies in many countries add a specific amount of fluoride to the water to ensure that citizens' teeth are protected from decay.

In the same way, homeopathic remedies work on the 'law of the minimum dose' to help the body regain its balance and so fight off any dis-ease it is suffering.

A homeopathic session

When attending a homeopathic practitioner, make sure you bring with you a record of any drugs you have been prescribed and remember to describe the nature of any pain you might be suffering. As mentioned earlier, the physical and psychological condition of the person will be taken into account and the person's personality plays a vital role in diagnosis. Therefore don't be surprised to find you are asked rather unusual questions such as:

Do you have any cravings?
What time of the day are you at your best?
What time of the day are you at your worst?
What type of weather do you prefer?
What type of food do you prefer?
What is your appetite like?
What type of fears do you have?
What are your audio preferences?

These questions are designed to find out what makes you tick, what your attitudes are and what affects you for good or ill. As no two people are alike, microdoses and remedies are specific to the individual, and the length of your treatment will depend on the specific diagnosis.

Whatever remedy you are prescribed it is important to remember not to handle the sugar-based pills themselves, and they should be sucked, not swallowed. Avoid minty toothpaste, coffee and peppermint, and wait for at least thirty minutes after taking the remedy before eating or drinking. Depending on your lifestyle the practitioner may initially prescribe a remedy to enable you to detoxify your body, to clear it of drugs, alcohol and other chemical substances.

When attending a session do not wear perfumes and avoid eating rich, spicy foods beforehand.

Where to find out more

Brunton, Dr Nelson, *Alternative Health, Homeopathy*, Optima, England, 1989.
Inglis, Brian, *Fringe Medicine*, Faber & Faber, 1968.

Reflexology

Reflexology is also known as zone therapy. It originated in ancient Eastern civilisations, and is one of the most natural forms of treatment for bringing the mind into harmony with the body. In this century North America USA ENT specialist Dr William M Fitzgerald codified ten zones of the body which are used by reflexologists today.

Philosophy of reflexology

The life force helps the body attain perfect balance and so function in harmony. When the natural flow of the life force is weakened, it allows waste matter to build up, clogging the natural balance and harmony.

The philosophy behind reflexology is that each foot 'reflects' the body, and therefore specific zones in each foot respond to specific organs or areas of the body.

By deeply massaging the reflexes of the feet the natural healing forces which are innate within each of us are stimulated to once again flow freely through the entire body.

How reflexology works

The feet are the microcosm of the body, the macrocosm.

In order to understand how reflexology works, you need to know that the body is divided into ten vertical zones and three horizontal zones. Both feet are then in turn divided into ten vertical and three horizontal zones, thus 'reflecting' the body zones.

These zones in the feet correspond exactly to the zones in the body and have been scaled down to the same proportion as that of a seated body. The top portion of the foot, ie the big toe, corresponds to the top of the head and the brain. As we move further down the foot we find the arm and shoulder corresponding with the portion just below the little toe, while the lower back is just in front of the heel. The left foot reflects the left part of the body, the right foot the right.

Illness develops when disharmony occurs because of weakened circulation of the life force flowing through the body. As it gets weaker a blockage of waste matter builds up and prevents the free flow of the vital forces necessary to life. When such blockage occurs in the body, this waste matter forms crystalline deposits which build up on the corresponding reflex zone on either or both feet.

By discovering through a manual examination where these crystalline deposits lie, the reflexologist can then diagnose the specific area of the body which is suffering the blockage.

For instance, if there is a crystalline deposit on the bottom of the heel of either foot, this could indicate a problem with the sciatic nerve. Therefore by massaging away this crystalline deposit the life force can once more flow freely through the body. With this newly attained flow the body and its organs renew themselves and can now work once again in harmony. In this case the problem with the sciatic nerve will be cured.

What reflexology can do for you

In life, cells grow and cells die, and as the body ages the balance between the growth and death of cells must be readjusted. For healthy living more cells must be growing than cells dying.

By undergoing a course of reflexology your body can maintain this balance and be revitalised because the reflexologist can stimulate slowed-down nerve and vascular systems, and boost blood circulation, which is essential for cell growth.

A session of reflexology

When you attend a reflexology session, the therapist will undertake two types of examination.

The first is a visual examination. By studying the formation of the foot and any bunions or corns which have developed, the therapist can tell what ailment is occurring in the corresponding part of the body.

The second examination is manual. By exerting finger pressure on the reflex zones, the therapist can discover where the crystalline deposits have built up. Any discomfort or pain which the person feels at this point is a warning signal that there is some complaint in the corresponding part of the body. The therapist will be able to diagnose by the depth of tenderness of the specific zone just how serious the problem is.

The reflexologist will have studied both anatomy and physiology, and these two examinations will result in an accurate reading of any disorder and its exact position within the body.

The final part of the session will comprise massage on the chosen reflex zones in order to break down the blockages of cystalline deposits which have been preventing the free flow of the life force. When these have been broken down the life force can flow freely through the body and the organs work in harmony once again.

The number of reflexology treatments needed will vary greatly, depending on the type of disorder and how long it has been in existence. The damaged or weak tissue which has been affected will be replaced, stimulated by reflexology. This recovery time, however, can vary according to the person and the ailment.

Where to find out more

Kunzdid, Kuiz, *Complete Guide to Foot Reflexology*, Thornson, England, 1984.
Carter, Mildred, *Helping Yourself with Foot Reflexology*, Prentice Hall, England, 1969.

Western Astrology

Have you ever wondered what motivates you to act as you do? Why on occasion you simply cannot get on with someone, no matter how you try, yet with others you become firm friends from the moment of your first meeting? Do you often wonder why one member of your family is so different from the others, why one shows a talent for the intellect, another for manual dexterity?

Every woman knows that she is affected physically by the moon, that her cycle of fertility waxes and wanes with the moon. But does she also feel psychologically affected by the lunar cycle?

We know that the tides are affected by the magnetic forces of the moon, and because the human body is made up of 70 per cent water, it makes sense to consider that we, too, are affected by the pull of the moon. We all use the word 'lunatic' which originally meant quite simply, 'affected by the moon'. Many of us are affected by mood swings, alert and all aware at the full moon, despondent and lacking in vitality as it wanes. And the influences of the other planets in the heavens may also exert a powerful influence on us.

In this Age of Aquarius a deeper interest in the astrological influence on our lives is quite understandable because this is the age of the independent thinker who is concerned with the betterment of the human condition. The typical Aquarian is committed to truth and innovation and can happily accept the twinning of technology and astrology.

You may be interested in finding out how you yourself have been influenced by your planetary signs. A knowledge of these influences and how they interact with others who have been born under different planetary signs can help people live more fulfilled lives. It can explain the interminable question of why a parent and child sometimes cannot get on and live in mutual misunderstanding and misery. It can explain why a student with the greatest education in the world would prefer to be a rock 'n' roll singer than choose a career in the 'professions' to the never-ending consternation of her parents. It can explain why at times we find ourselves in situations and environments in which we feel completely out of place, and why we feel so much at home with certain people and places.

Although people often laugh at the idea of following their stars, today most popular newspapers and magazines have a section devoted to the Occidental or Western Zodiac, which shows just how many people do take astrology even half seriously! It is calculated that in the USA alone 32,000,000 people have some belief in astrology.

There is no need to fear the effects of astrology on your life. Instead you can welcome it because astrology can tell you what is possible and when, depending on the position of the planets.

This knowledge does not impel you to follow a particular path. You are always in control of your actions because your will is your own.

A brief history of astrology

Early people were dependent on the heavens. Consider how fearsome it must have been for Stone Age peoples to survive, eternal victims of the sun, the moon, the tides, the elements.

It's not surprising that they looked to what was above them, the stars, for help. They saw how the elements changed with the movement of the sun and the moon. How crops grew and flourished as spring became summer. How important it was to harvest the growth in autumn before the winter solstice forced all growing things into months of hibernation. It was no wonder they thought of the planets as gods.

More than 5,000 years ago Megalithic people built one of the oldest astronomical monuments in the world, at Newgrange, on the east coast of Ireland. Here on the day of the winter solstice (which means 'standing sun') the waning sun strikes an exact point to throw light on the Sun God. What extraordinary knowledge and commitment to their beliefs they must have had to build such an enduring monument with such precision! Some years later, in southern England, the Bronze Age people, known as the Beakers, built their own monument to the stars, Stonehenge.

In 2,500 BC on the banks of the Nile the Egyptians constructed their pyramids which not only housed their Pharaohs but also provided perfect viewing points for astronomers. The Chaldeans, a mixed race of Assyrians and Babylonians, were famous for their knowledge of astrology and enhanced the Egyptians' interest in the science. It was possibly they who advised on the design of the pyramids, which were then built by Egyptian slaves. The Israelites, fleeing from slavery in Egypt, brought their knowledge of astrology to a wider audience as they wandered across the European mainland and beyond.

Astrology is a deductive process whereby the movements of the astral bodies across the sky were observed and recorded year after year. From these records certain predictions were possible. Until the birth of rationalism in the seventeenth century, astrology and astronomy went hand in hand; they are both the study of the influence of extra-terrestrial life forces.

Originally an astrological chart would be drawn up only for the Chief of state, the Pharaoh or Emperor. Such a chart would be a record of the planets as they moved through the heavens, and from it the astrologer would predict their influence on wars, storms, floods, and drought. There is an example of this on the tomb of the Egyptian Pharaoh Rameses VI, who lived around 1200 BC. Here there is an engraving of a star map showing the culminations of the stars for each hour of the night throughout the year.

The Greeks learned astrology from a Babylonian astrologer, Berosus, and it was they who popularised the personal birth chart which calculates individual destinies dependent on an individual's moment of birth. Ptolemy, the Greek astronomer, wrote an astrological textbook, the *Tetrabiblos* in about 120 AD, and his records have been little changed to this day. The Roman emperors surrounded themselves with their own personal astrologers, although the popularity of astrology depended on the particular beliefs of the ruler of the time. The Emperor Augustus, for instance, struck coinage with his birthsign, Capricorn, on it and even allowed his horoscope to be published, predicting the date of his death. Julius Caesar had a new calendar drawn up by his astrologer and this calendar, with a 'leap year' every fourth year, we still use today.

With the fall of Rome astrology lost its popularity and was kept alive mainly through underground interest. It began to surface again in the Middle Ages, with notable writers such as Chaucer, Dante, Shakespeare, Goethe and St Thomas Aquinas recording their interest in it. With the beginning of rationalism in the seventeenth century astrology was once more relegated to underground interest.

At the turn of the twentieth century in the USA, Evangeline Adams became notorious when she correctly predicted negative influences affecting a hotelier whose premises burned to the ground after he had ignored her warning. She was taken to court as a fortune teller, which at that time was against the law, but by using her predictive powers correctly she was hailed by the judge for her ability, and set free. Since then, all kinds of eminent and notable people have found astrology valid and helpful and its popularity in the West has grown phenomenally.

The celestial zodiac and you

Looking at the zodiacal wheel you can see that the birth chart is divided into several sections and shows many symbols. To find out how your life is ruled astrologically you need to study not only the twelve signs of the zodiac, but also their qualities, the ten planets which rule them and the twelve houses into which these planets fall.

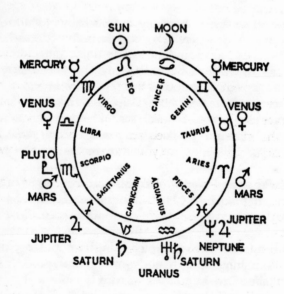

The twelve signs of the zodiac

The Chaldeans observed and recorded the path of their gods Sin (the Moon) and Shamash (the Sun) through the heavens. The constellations they passed were taken as marker points to the movement of the planets and the twelve specific constellations were given names which have survived to this day. These are Sun signs, so-named because the energy of the sun enters into these signs on specific dates. The sun sign is the image you present to the world, while the ascendant (the sign rising in the eastern horizon at the moment of birth), is the true self. The ascendant has to be calculated first when making up a birth chart, and it is from this position that the other signs fall into place.

To work out a full birth or natal chart for yourself, either go to a reputable astrologer, or use the list of recommended books and chart shown at the end of this section.

A professional astrologer will be versed not only in the intricacies of casting your birth chart, but also in the extremely important task of interpreting it correctly.

By plotting your birth chart and interpreting the detail given, an astrologer can advise you on certain areas of your life which require more attention, which areas should be encouraged or suppressed, what career path you should follow, what character traits you should look for in a partner, how best to understand your children, etc. The expert can also, by studying the transit of the planets through the heavens within the following month or year, advise you on which path to follow, which path to leave.

Whatever the astrologer tells you, however, remember that although the stars are destined for certain fixed paths in the heavens, the choice of the path you take is open to your own free will.

In order to draw up a full birth chart, an astrologer needs the hour, date and place of your birth. With these facts the astrologer would use an Ephemeris, which is a detailed record of all the positions of the planets relating to different points on the Earth, in order to calculate the exact position of each of the planets at the individual's time of birth. The precise time and place of birth is essential to achieve an accurate reading.

However, if you want to find out just basic characteristics of yourself of your friends, the following is a brief guide.

First, find out the zodiac sign under which you were born, by recalling your birth date:

Zodiac Sign	Dates	Symbol	Glyph
1. Aries:	21 March-19 April	the Ram	♈
2. Taurus:	20 April-20 May	the Bull	♉
3. Gemini	21 May-21 June	the Twins	♊
4. Cancer:	22 June-22 July	the Crab	♋
5. Leo:	3 July-22 August	the Lion	♌
6. Virgo:	23 August-22 September	the Virgin	♍
7. Libra:	23 September-23 October	the Scales	♎
8. Scorpio:	24 October-21 November	the Scorpion	♏
9. Sagittarius:	2 November-21 December	the Archer	♐
10 Capricorn	2 December-19 January	the Goat	♑
11 Aquarius:	20 January-18 February	the Waterbearer	♒
12 Pisces:	19 February-20 March	the Fish	♓

Psychological types of the zodiac signs

These are divided into three groupings: Positivity and Negativity, the Triplicities and the Quadruplicities.

1. Positivity and negativity
Positive in astrology means extroversion and self-expression. Negative means introversion and passivity. Starting with Aries,

which is positive, and going on to Taurus which is negative, the signs are then alternately positive and negative. (Positive signs are those with odd numbers, negative those with even.).

2. The Triplicities
These are also known as the Elements, and are divided into Fire, Earth, Air and Water, as follows:

Fire (Aries, Leo, Sagittatius):
Firey characteristics which burn bright with enthusiasm and often burn up the opposition when faced with power struggles. Firey people feel strongly about things.

Earth (Taurus, Virgo, Capricorn):
These practical people have a more restrained 'down to earth' attitude towards life. Earth people are concerned with sensations.

Air (Gemini, Libra, Aquarius):
'Airy, fairy' people cannot be contained, are always on the move both physically and mentally. Air people are great thinkers.

Water (Cancer, Scorpio, Pisces):
'Still waters run deep' and these characters are emotional and intuitive. Water people are guided by their deep intuition.

3. The Quadruplicities (or qualities)
These are common characteristics possessed by people affected by the same sign. There are three such signs: Cardinal, Fixed and Mutable.

Cardinal signs (Aries, Cancer, Libra, Capricorn)
These are the instigators of new, innovative ideas, people who 'do' rather than 'talk' about how things should be done. They create things and get things moving, but need others with Fixed or Mutable qualities to actually see things through, while they go off and create something else.

Fixed signs (Taurus, Leo, Scorpio, Aquarius)
These people are often resistant to change but follow things through, often to the bitter end, and can be relied upon for loyalty and steadfast courage. When attached to an innovative

sign such as Aquarius it can mean someone who is determined to see a unique innovation through, who won't take 'no' for an answer.

Mutable signs (Gemini, Virago Sagittarius, Pisces)
These people are adaptable and therefore able to cope with sudden changes and set-backs. They make good diplomats or representatives, working as 'go-betweens' to create harmony between the Cardinal and Fixed signs.

Physiological connections with the zodiac
Just as the heavens affect our psychology, so they affect our physiology. Astrological medicine was first written about by the Greeks, although its existence originated before that time. As Aries is the first sign of the Zodiac, it corresponds with the head. Arians, therefore are often affected by headache and migraine. The physiological correspondence of each sign is shown under the interpretation of the signs.

The divisions on the birth chart

Before placing the planets in the signs, there are two very important divisions which must be placed on the birth chart.
The first is a horizontal line which cuts across the chart and shows the position of the rising Sun at the time of your birth. This is known as the Ascendant and shows the position at 6.00am, while the Descendant, the opposite point of this line, shows the Sun's position at 6.00pm. If the majority of planets are above the Ascendant/ Descendant line this shows an outgoing personality, while if they are below it you are more likely to be introverted.
The second division is the vertical line which cuts the chart from top to bottom. The topmost point, known as the Mid Heaven, shows the position of the sun at noon on the day of your birth, while the bottom or Nadir point shows the Sun's position at midnight.
Basically, we can see that if the majority of the planets are placed left of the mid heaven/nadir division you are more likely to be independent, while if they are to the right it means you have to work harder to control your own destiny.

88

The ten planets

Planets are our sources of energy, each planet representing principles unique to that planet. Each sign is ruled by a particular planet, and takes on the qualities of that planet. It is thought that the qualities of our zodiac sign is the conscious face we show the world, while the qualities of the planet which rules us is our sub-conscious.

As each planet travels through the heavens it is in 'transit' or passes in and out of each of our twelves houses, through our houses. So each planet influences us in different ways. It is, in fact, from these positions and movements of planets as seen from our position on earth that interpretations and predictions are made in astrology.

Once we know what effect each planet will have on us as it moves through each of our 'houses', we can use this knowledge to our advantage by taking decisive action, or perhaps by taking no action at all and 'lying low'. In this way we can take control of our lives, instead of passively accepting outside influences over which we may have felt we have little or no control. Understanding in advance the predestined influences at work for or against us enables us to use our free will to choose the most fruitful path. You will not be able to discover where the planets were in the heavens at the time of your birth until you have your own personal birth chart drawn up.

There are ten planets in all, each of which (with the exception of the Sun and the Moon), is named after one of the Roman or Greek gods.

The Sun:
The outward expression of our purpose in life. Positive, egoistic, creative and outgoing.
The Moon:
The unconscious, inner self, emotional and imaginative, intuitive and sensitive.
Mercury:
The sign of communication, quickwittedness and creative logic Excelling in self-expression and diplomacy.
Venus:
Love of beautiful things, and love of people. A sense of refinement and harmonious living.

Mars:
Energetic and responsive in business and personal life. Quick to act and often quick to join battle.

Jupiter:
The pursuit of knowledge, expansion of the mind through philosophy, spirituality and perhaps religion.

Saturn:
Solidity and reliability, self-disciplined and constructive. Sometimes inhibited in self expression which, with patience, can be overcome.

Uranus:
Dynamic, quick, humanitarian and inventive. Hates any restriction, fights for freedom and can sometimes be eccentric.

Neptune:
Artistically creative and deeply spiritual. Can be interested in spiritualism and mysticism.

Pluto:
Flair for business and for starting again after being knocked down. Possible leaning towards addictive substances.

A brief interpretation of each sign

Aries, the Ram (Positive, Fire, Cardinal) Ruled by Mars.
The Arian is assertive, pioneering, enterprising, demanding. This is the first sign of the Zodiac and the bearer always wants to be first, sometimes to the detriment of others.

Physiologically, the area affected by Aries is the head, and Arians often suffer from unexplained headaches and migraine.

The Arian is compatible with Saggitarians and Leos.

Taurus, the Bull (Negative, Earth, Fixed) Ruled by Venus.
The Taurean is practical, reliable, person and warm-hearted. This is the sign of steadfastness to both opinions and roots, so a stable home environment is important, and the Taurean usually prefers to live in the country.

The physiological area of the Taurean is the throat and neck.

The Taurean is compatible with Capricorns and Virgoans

Gemini, the Twins (Positive, Air, Mutable). Ruled by Mercury.
The most adaptable, versatile sign of the Zodiac, the twins are witty and communicative, and have a flair for words and

language. Geminians can appear unstable as they have a low threshold for boredom and quickly change their minds.

The lungs and chest are the physiological areas of the Geminian.

Geminians are compatible with Aquarians and Librans.

Cancer, the Crab (Negative, Water, Cardinal) Ruled by the Moon.

Cancerians have a strong parental instinct, can be kind and sympathetic, thrifty and shrewd. Like the crab, the Cancerian shows a tough exterior to the outside world but is soft inside. Can be easily hurt and tends towards self-pity.

The physiological areas ruled by Cancer are the breasts and the stomach.

Cancerians are compatible with Pisceans and Scorpions.

Leo, the Lion (Positive, Fire, Fixed) Ruled by the Sun.

The Leonine character is positive, outgoing, generous and creative. Leos, whose ruling planet is the Sun, love to shine at whatever they do and are often found literally centre-stage as actors or media personalities. Like the lion, Leos are natural leaders but can often be bossy and intolerant.

Physiologically the area ruled by Leo is the heart.

Leos are compatible with Saggitarians and Arians.

Virgo, the Virgin (Negative, Earth, Mutable) Ruled by Mercury.

Virgoans are meticulous in their dress and in their work. There is no better slogger than this mutable earth personality who will analyse a problem down to the finest detail, sometimes to the detriment of creativity and innovation. A Virgoan is the perfect employee, punctual, tidy and loyal.

The abdomen and intestines are the physiological areas ruled by Virgo.

Virgoans are compatible with Capricorns and Taureans.

Libra, the Scales (Positive, Air, Cardinal) Ruled by Venus.

Balance is essential for the Libran who is doomed or blessed to see both sides of a problem, and so often finds it difficult to make a decision. Self-expression is essential for the Libran to maintain balance, so care should be taken in choosing the right career and the right partner in emotional relationships.

The kidneys and lumbar region are ruled by Libra.

The Libran is compatible with Aquarians and Geminians.

Scorpio, the Scorpion (Negative, Water, Fixed) Ruled by Pluto.
The Scorpion was the symbol of Ishtar, the goddess of love, so it's no wonder Scorpions are known for their deep passions, especially sexual. They are also passionately secretive and determined to get what they want, even if it means resorting to underhand ways of achieving their aims. This persistence can prove a positive trait, however, if the Scorpion is on your side.
The physiological areas governed by Scorpio are the genitals, the bladder and the rectum.
Scorpions are compatible with Cancerians and Pisceans.

Sagittarius, the Archer (Positive, Fire, Mutable) Ruled by Jupiter.
This Archer is happy to shoot an arrow from a bow and follow it regardless, for to Saggitarians the meaning of life is adventure. They are natural explorers and follow the dictum 'It is better to travel hopefully than to arrive'. Optimistic and always curious, Saggitarians are easily bored and not always responsible.
Physiologically, Sagittarius rules the hips and the thighs.
The Sagittarian is compatible with Leos and Arians.

Capricorn, the Goat (Negative, Earth, Cardinal) Ruled by Saturn.
There are two kinds of goat, the first scales mountains and, no matter how rough the terrain, always lands safely, while the domestic goat is reserved, restricted by a short chain. The first is ambitious, with strong aspirations, the latter is calculating and cautious, but both are imaginative and thorough.
The physiological areas governed by Capricorn are the knees.
Capricorns are compatible with Virgos and Taureans.

Aquarius, the Water Bearer (Positive, Air, Fixed) Ruled by Uranus.
The Water-Bearer encourages the free flow of original thought and expression. The most well-rounded sign of the Zodiac, Aquarians are helpful, understanding and very idealistic, shielding the underdog and rebelling against injustice. While saving the world in general, their need for independence can make them seem detached, and they often stay away from intimate relationships.

Physiologically the calves and ankles are ruled by Aquarius. Aquarians are compatible with Geminians and Librans.

Pisces, the Fish (Negative, Water, Mutable) Ruled by Neptune.
The most creative sign of the Zodiac, Pisceans are a mixture of all the other signs. They are the most intuitive and, while feeling deeply, often find it difficult to express themselves unless in writing. The Piscean needs the help of a mentor to develop self-confidence, and would do well to keep away from addictive substances which could hinder true creativity.

The feet are governed physiologically by Pisces.

Pisceans are compatible with Scorpions and Cancerians.

The Houses

The birth or birth chart, showing the twelve signs, their qualities and the position of each of the ten planets, is divided into twelve equal wedges of 30 degrees each. These are the Houses, each of which defines a specific area of life experience from childhood to adulthood, from social abilities to business acumen. You will find that some of these Houses may be empty of any planets, others may have two or three. The planets are placed within the chart based on their location at the time of the individual's birth, therefore the true meaning of the planets is affected by its position within the Houses.

Taking the Birth Chart as a clock, the First House begins at 6.00am, sunrise, while the Twelfth House begins at 4.00am and ends just before 6.00am.

First House: Describes the personality and personal interests of the individual.
Second House: Personal security and attitude towards personal possessions.
Third House: Communication and travel, ability to relate to society and family.
Fourth House: Early domestic and family life, investments for the future.
Fifth House: Pleasures of family, friendships and the joys of living.
Sixth House: Attitude towards work and work colleagues, conformity to society and personal health.
Seventh House: Partnerships in marriage and business, how you

relate to legal documentation and requirements.

Eighth House: Income and inheritance, attitude towards other people's money.

Ninth House: Travel, new horizons, far off visions and interest in intellectual studies such as philosophy and religion.

Tenth House: Career ambitions, social status and reputation.

Eleventh House: Friends and social life, identification with group aims and personal ambition.

Twelfth House: House of self-undoing, solitude and escapism.

The Aspects

Now the astrologer knows which planet is in which sign, and which planet is in which House, so the next stage is to discover the Aspects, the angular distance measured in degrees between two planets in the heavens as seen from your position on earth.

These Aspects can have a positive, negative, powerful or weak effect on the elements in your chart. The main Aspects are as follows:

Conjunction A joining of forces between two planets which are zero degrees apart or just a few degrees apart.

Opposition These planets are 180 degrees opposite each other and this means they have a negative, opposing force against each other.

Sextile When two planets are 60 degrees apart it indicates an opportunity for them to have a positive influence on one another.

Square When two planets are 90 degrees apart it means the two planets work at cross-purposes to each other.

Trine When two planets are 120 degrees apart it symbolises a positive aspect where there is an opportunity for good fortune.

Where to find out more

Parker, Julia and Derek, *The Complete Astrologer*, McGraw Hill, New York, 1971. Pelletier, Robert and Leonard Cataldo, *Be Your Own Astrologer*, Pan Books, London, 1984.

Mayo, Jeff, *Teach Yourself Astrology*, Hodder & Stoughton, England, 1964.

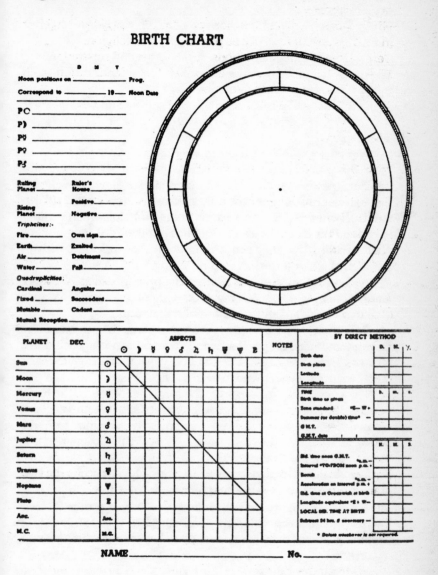

BIRTH CHART

Noon positions on _____ Prog.

Correspond to _____ 19— Noon Date

PC _____

P) _____

P⚥ _____

P♀ _____

P♂ _____

Ruling Planet _____ Ruler's House _____

Rising Planet _____ Positive _____

Triplicities:- Negative _____

Fire _____ Own sign _____

Earth _____ Exalted _____

Air _____ Detriment _____

Water _____ Fall _____

Quadruplicities:

Cardinal _____ Angular _____

Fixed _____ Succeedent _____

Mutable _____ Cadent _____

Mutual Reception _____

PLANET	DEC.	ASPECTS	NOTES
		☉) ☿ ♀ ♂ ♃ ♄ ♅ ♆ ♇	
Sun	☉		
Moon	)		
Mercury	☿		
Venus	♀		
Mars	♂		
Jupiter	♃		
Saturn	♄		
Uranus	♅		
Neptune	♆		
Pluto	♇		
Asc.	Asc.		
M.C.	M.C.		

BY DIRECT METHOD

	D.	M.	Y.
Birth date			
Birth place			
Latitude			
Longitude			

TIME	h.	m.	s.
Birth time as given			
Zone standard *E— W*			
Summer (or double) time* —			
G.M.T.			
G.M.T. date			

	H.	M.	S.
Sid. time noon G.M.T.			
Interval *TO/FROM* noon p.m. +			
Result			
Acceleration on interval p.m. +			
Sid. time at Greenwich at birth			
Longitude equivalent *E + W —*			
LOCAL SID. TIME AT BIRTH			
Subtract 24 hrs. if necessary —			

* Delete whichever is not required.

NAME _____ No. _____

Divining by Dice

A brief background to dice throwing

No one knows when fortune telling by dice was first developed, but excavations of prehistoric sites have uncovered astragali, the knucklebones of animals such as goats and sheep, with marks engraved on them. These are the first numbered dice and show that divining by the throw of the dice or casting lots was possibly the oldest form of fortune telling.

Archaeologists have discovered Egyptian artefacts of chance dating back to 3,500 BC, together with many records of wall paintings of games still in existence in their tombs.

In Roman mythology the god Mercury was the patron of dice players and according to legend his winged sandals were called Talaria, from the Latin *talus* for heel. The Romans called dice 'tali' because they were made from the heel bones of animals.

There are many references to the throwing of lots in the Bible, specifically in the Book of Proverbs of the Old Testament which allows 'Though the lot is thrown, the decision is wholly from the Lord', as well as in the New Testament where the Roman guards threw lots for the clothes of Christ.

The Roman Emperor Claudius wrote a book on dice games, which shows how popular and acceptable dice throwing was to the Roman. In the thirteenth century the French writer Richard de Fournival wrote a poem about the 216 separate ways of throwing three dice, and this sum has never been proved incorrect.

With the introduction of card games and horseracing from the seventeenth century onwards, the popularity of dice games began to decline. Nowadays dice are more popular for board-games such as backgammon, snakes & ladders and monopoly. However, just because dice throwing has been overshadowed by board and computer games, it need not stop you from trying your luck with the stones.

How to tell your fortune

All you need is a set of three dice, one red, one white and one green. To throw the three dice use your cupped hands or some form of beaker. Below is a brief explanation of what each numbered dice means. Keep a pen and paper handy to jot down each throw, and then you can take your time interpreting them.

The Red stands for 100s, White stands for 10s and the Green for single digits. Throw the three dice together, and jot down the numbers beginning with Red, then White,then Green.

To read a basic fortune, throw the three dice three times. This is what each throw stands for:

First -will answer the questioner's general situation.
Second-will answer the questioner's financial and business
   situation.
Third-will answer the questioner's situation regarding
  love and affection.

So if your first throw is a Red 3, a White 6 and a Green 2, you have cast the number 362. If on the second throw you get a Red 4, a White 3 and a Green 1, you have 431. Then throw the dice for the last time.

Using the keyword guide below you can interpret your fortune on a simple level. Any interpretation will depend on the attitude and circumstances of the questioner. For instance, the throw of dice may be the same for a 20 year old student of French literature and a 50 year old banking executive but will have a much different interpretation. The keyword guide is at most basic level. If you would like to find out more about dice divination, the short list of books on the subject at the end of this chapter will guide you.

What the dice mean

Red (hundreds)
6 Bat
Symbolises a shadow which is hiding good and evil a warning to beware and not take things at face value.
5 Beetle
Single minded purposefulness. Fulfilling ambitions.
4 Horseshoe
Good fortune, success and happiness. The horseshoe has protection values against loss and evil.
3 Boat
The symbol for movement, travel, following a quest, receiving messages from afar and communications.
2 Skull
Sudden unexpected situations. Change by transformations.
1 Web
Symbolises entanglements, blinded by illusion and involvement not always welcome.

White (tens)
6 Crossroads
Hidden surprises, decisions to be made, strangers coming into your family/environment and causing contentions.
5 Cat
Home, family, relationships, relatives, children and marriage.
4 Knife
A warning of intrigues, danger from making decisions too quickly, tension and deceit.
3 Heart
Illumination and happiness, love and friendship.
2 Stork
An omen of new beginnings and inventiveness, an omen of ingenuity.
1 Sun
Dynamism, ambition, energy, success and power.

Green (tens)
6 Fruit Tree
Reward for hard work. Abundance, money, property and possessions.
5 Goblet

Friendship, prudence, celebration. Search for the unattainable.
4 Key
Access to knowledge, door opening and closing, opportunities offered, answers to questions.
3 Ladder
Ways to achieve, the choice is in your hands, ambition and enthusiasm.
2 Lightning
Move fast, act quickly, unexpected danger/anger is turned against you.
1 Snail
Take care, move slowly and make no decisions. Slow down and be on guard.

Examples of a dice game

Example 1
Take an example of a throw which gives the questioner the numbers 621 (Bat/Stork/Snail). The following is a simplified reading of what 621 might mean:

Throw 1: general situation.
On the surface things are going alright but be careful Don't overstretch yourself. You're full of ideas and ready for something new. Slow down. Take time to make decisions.

Throw 2: business and financial situation.
You are full of good ideas and fortune will smile on you if you don't make any quick decision and make sure to examine proposals carefully.

Throw 3: love and affection.
Slow down and relax with loved ones. Make plans together for the future.

Example 2
For this example we assume that the throw was 336, giving a reading of Boat/Heart/Fruit Tree. This again is a simplified example of what it might mean:

Throw 1: general situation.

Plan a visit to an old friend. It will repay you with some form of reward, perhaps inner happiness.

Throw 2: business and financial situation.
A business venture abroad should be looked after, and might prove successful.

Throw 3: love and affection.
Tell the people you love that you care for them, and show your care with a suitable present. It will make everyone feel good.

There can be different variations in the meanings of these throws depending on the situation of the questioner.

Where to find out more

Line, Julia and David, *Fortune Telling by Dice*, Aquarian Press, England, 1984
King, Francis X, *The Encyclopaedia of Fortune Telling*, Octupus Books, London, England, 1988.

Graphology

When you read a hand-written letter or note from people you have never been in contact with before do you find yourself making assumptions about their character which can turn out to be very accurate when you get to know them better? When writing by hand yourself, do you notice a slight variation in the script depending on the content of the message or your knowledge of the recipient? This reaction is quite normal because handwriting is a physical expression of inner emotions. It is the image you present to the rest of the world and is as individual as a person's fingerprint.

The philosophy behind graphology

Graphology is the study of handwriting. 'Graph' is the Greek word for 'writing' and 'ology' means 'science'.

The science of graphology can be divided into the work of a graphologist and the work of a handwriting analyst. Whichever path is chosen, the science is based on the philosophy that the art of writing is an extension of the inner self, a mirror image of how we feel emotionally and physically, how we act, our innermost motives. When we write each stroke we make is controlled by the mind, which then sends a message to the nerves which in turn motivate our muscles in order for our hand to form the script. The script we form expresses our sub-conscious feelings in the extension, the speed and the pressure we use in writing.

Therefore it follows that if one's mind is in uncontrollable turmoil it will create uncontrolled, confused script, while if it is at peace it will create smooth script.

The work of the graphologist
The graphologist studies handwriting in order to interpret a person's character and personality. By analysing the emotions,

the motivation, the capabilities and the face we show to society the graphologist can help individuals or businesses decide on the advisability of partnership or employment with people about whom they know little. A graphologist can also indicate energy levels and diagnose some types of mental and physical illness, such as depression and heart problems.

The work of the handwriting analyst
The handwriting analyst, on the other hand, studies only the lines and physical structure of the writing in order to gauge the authenticity of a script. The emotions and motivations of the writer do not come into this analysis. A handwriting analyst is employed by all sorts of legal and judicial authorities world-wide to report on the authenticity of artworks, wills, and other legal documentation. Some police forces ask for a handwriting expert's help in analysing the script of one who writes letters for reason of threat, blackmail or ransom.

A short history of graphology
Although in the year 500 BC Confucius warned his subjects to be careful of one whose writing 'sways as the reed in the wind', and Roman statesmen such as Julius Caesar and Cicero (around 100 BC) believed in character analysis through handwriting, graphology did not become widespread until the mid seventeenth century.

It was in the 1870s that the Frenchman Abbé Michon rediscovered the first book on handwriting written by Professor Baldo from Bologna, around 1630. Abbé Michon created the word 'graphology' when he published a book on the new science which is now a classic. This in turn stimulated interest in graphology right across Europe and influenced writers and artists of the period.

Graphology has become an accepted form of analysis right across the globe. Handwriting analysts are licensed to testify in court matters. Large companies frequently ask applicants to send, along with their job application, a hand-written sample so that a graphologist can analyse the person's abilities and motivations.

Analysing a sample of handwriting
Obviously it is good to analyse a sample of handwriting which

has been written without any self-consciousness, such as a letter to a friend.

If this is not available, a subject can be asked to write a sample for you to read, which should be at least a half-page in length if not a full page. The topic or content of the writing should be chosen carefully so as to include words for which some form of emotion is felt. An example might include a critique on a recently seen TV or radio programme or perhaps a film or play. Other subjects might be the writer's views on career, or personal goals for the future.

It is important that the sample of handwriting you choose to analyse is obtained under certain conditions. For instance, the writer should be sitting in a comfortable position in a friendly environment, and have a choice of ballpoint pen or fountain pen. The paper used should be white, of standard size and unlined. A few sheets should be offered to the writer.

You should also find out the writer's age group, the sex and country of origin or education. This is because the teaching of writing in primary school differs from country to country and can therefore have a bearing on the originality of the writing in mature years.

Make certain that any sample of writing you obtain includes the writer's signature. The reason for this will be explained later.

It would be useful, if possible, to get access to a sample of the person's writing carried out some time earlier. This can reveal important changes in the personality and character of the writer over time.

General points

In the United States of America the majority of school children are taught the Palmer Method of writing, while in English-speaking Western Europe children are generally taught the Spencerian Method. It therefore follows that when analysing a sample by someone who has written in a language other than the mother-tongue this should be taken into consideration.

If the writer has made a conscious decision to be left-handed (ie is not writing with left hand due to accident with right hand), then there is no difference when reading a sample. Some examples may look awkward and forced. This would show a character trait of someone who stubbornly goes against the tide. If the writer is confortable using the left hand then it will not look awkward.

Writing characteristics have both a positive and a negative pole. The positive or negative characteristic of the graphological sample is interpreted by the overall impression of the writing sample. This interpretation takes into consideration the spaces between lines, the natural flow and the originality of the script. Unless stated, the negative characteristic is the opposite of the positive characteristic shown.

The general spread

Before studying the handwriting, first of all look at the spread of the piece. Observe the use of margins, the ascent or descent of the flow of writing and the spaces left between words and lines.

Are there generous margins to right and left, or does the writing take over the entire page? Is there space left for margins above and below the writing?

Wide margins to left and right of the page shows a character who is generous with both time and money. One who leaves little or no margins is aware of wastage and thinks before acting. A script which leaves a wide margin to the left but little or no margin to the right symbolises someone who is naturally impulsive and generous but tries to curb extravagance. The opposite, a narrow left margin and a wide right margin, shows a natural thriftiness with an effort towards generosity. Mixed margins shows someone who is inconsistent and unable to curb natural generosity.

Does the writing follow an invisible horizontal line (or base line) across the page or does it ascend or descend as the flow continues? Writing which has a tendency to ascend shows an optimistic, enthusiastic character. That with a downward trend mirrors a cautious, pessimistic nature. A mixture of ascending and descending script warns of a temperamental person who is governed by extremes of behaviour. Script running horizontally along the baseline shows a realistic, cool-headed person.

Is there generous space left between words, and enough space allowed to 'read between the lines', or is it cramped and confused? A wide space between the lines shows detachment and formality. It can also symbolise isolation. Writing which is narrow and leaves little space between words or lines shows economy, secrecy or instability. A proportionately spaced script shows gregariousness and sociability. Confused writing is a mirror image of one with a confused mind who is incapable of self-expression. When you see a thoroughly illegible script it is a sign that the writer does not wish 'to be read' by anyone. In this case the question is, what is the writer hiding?

The script and letters

Now let's look at the details of the script. There are certain important aspects to take into account before we can study individual letters.

Firstly let's look at the **zones**. There are three zones: the upper, middle and lower. In simple terms these can be related to the human body.

The upper zone is the super-ego, the intellect and the spirit. Think of this as showing the head and brain of the subject. The middle is the ego and the way in which we relate to society. Think of this as the torso. The lower zone is the id, the realm of instinct and sensuality and materialism. This can be related to our sexual organs and how we instinctively move in life.

When looking at a specimen of writing, see if the loops of the upper zone (for instance the letters l, b and h), and lower zones (for instance g, j, y) are full or lean, and if the letters in the middle zone are full or lean. Each element will tell you about the person's attitude to intellect, to the ego and to the id.

The upper zone: this shows the intellect of the writer. A full or looped letter shows imaginative thoughts and speech, perhaps a day-dreamer and one who enjoys following intellectual pursuits. A leanness shows an analytical mind and rational thought.

The middle zone: this is the writer's ego and the attitude to society in general. A full, generous letter shows sociability and amiability. A lean middle zone shows emotional control and social discrimination, and inhibition.

The lower zone: this shows the instincts and sexual libido of the writer, the people and things which are of consequence. A full, looped lower zone can show strong sexual imagination. An unfinished loop can mean a disturbance in the sex life, and no loop at all can show fatalism and sexual sublimation.

The next important general factor to take into consideration is the direction in which the writing slants. Judge this slant by imagining a horizontal line running under the script. Writing slanting between 60º-85º is considered leftward, writing at 85º-95º is considered vertical, and writing at 145º is considered rightward.

Left slanting script symbolises the ego, the past and introversion. The person who writes with this type of script

105

could be interpreted as an introvert who holds a strong belief in tradition, is cautious and self-controlled, whose head rules the heart.

Vertical script symbolises independence and neutrality. One who writes with a vertical script can be rational, uncommitted and independent of thought. It also shows self-control and perhaps rigidity.

Right slanting script symbolises the attitude towards society. This person would be an extrovert, sociable and passionate, who has a radical streak and could be emotionally extravagant.

Now let's look at the **size**, **regularity** and **pressure** of the script.

The **size** shows the self-image of the writer. If it is a large script the writer has a positive self-image, is self-reliant and can be extravagant, believing in doing things the right way. Extra-large script shows extremes, the exhibitionist who needs to be noticed at all costs. Small script shows a modest self-image with traits of tolerance, timidity and single-mindedness.

The **regularity** of the script covers the regularity of slant, height and distance of upper and lower zone strokes. A writer with a regular script has endurance, is stable and orderly. One showing irregularity is emotional, impulsive and open-minded.

The **pressure** shows the energy of the writer. Pressure in a regular script can show endurance, steadiness and possibly obstinacy. Pressure in an irregular script can symbolise vitality, impulsiveness and aggressiveness.

Lack of pressure can symbolise lack of energy and lack of libido. If there is lack of pressure in a regular script this shows the writer to be adaptable or lacking resistance. Lack of pressure in an irregular script shows impressionability, sensitivity or weakness.

Now we look at the **connectedness** of the script. Connectedness is where letters are joined together without a break. A connected script is where five or more letters are written in one go without a break (except where there is an i to dot or a t to cross). Connected script symbolises sociability, quick-thinking and intelligence.

Where there are only four or less letters written in one stroke, this is disconnected script. Disconnected script symbolises individualism, independence and intuitive thinking.

Differing from connectedness are **connections**. Connections are where individual letters are connected to one another in joined script. To study the four different types of connections you need to look at the letters n, m, h where they join other letters.

There are four main connections known as arcade, garland, angular and thready.

A. *and then*   h n

B. *and then*   h n

C. *and then*   n h

D. *and then she*   m h

```
A = Arcade
B = Angular
C = Garland
D = Thready
```

The arcade connection shows reserve, tact, and possibly distrust.

The garland indicates frankness, kindness and possibly indifference.

The angular concerns resistance, firmness and coldness.

The thready connection shows flexibility, diplomacy or cunning.

Individual letters

Capital or initial letters are those used in the script to begin paragraphs and sentences. As they are the first letter they show how the person reacts to new beginnings.

Lead-ins, a stroke used before the main body of the letter, show dependency on others and a need to cling to the past and convention. Someone who writes without any lead-ins has eliminated unnecessary tradition and convention, and shows a willingness to solve problems without procrastination.

Final letters are those which come at the end of the sentence. They can slope upwards, downwards or can be flattened out. An up-sloping final shows a sociable person who enjoys and needs company. A down-sloping final indicates a judgmental character who can be moralistic and cruel, while a flattened out final shows a generous person who will see a project through to the end.

The letter l is one of the most important as is stands for the ego, for the leader, for Number 1. A plain capital l without any additions shows a sense of the essentials, of discarding anything unnecessary. An l with flats top and bottom symbolises someone with cultural interests, while a looped upper zone shows strong egoism and greed.

The small i can have its dot: to the left showing caution, exactly above which symbolises precision, to the right impulsiveness and enthusiasm, and if its dot is missing this shows unreliability and carelessness. Where the dot is placed high it shows idealism, where low realism. Where the dot is faint it signifies poor vitality, where it forms a circle, escapism.

The letter T symbolises attitudes. A capital T with a bar on top which is equally balanced shows a straightforward, balanced personality. Where the top bar is extended to the right it indicates protectiveness, and where it ascends upwards from left to right this shows a strong streak of ambition.

In lower case t, where the bar is highly placed above the upstand this signifies idealism, where it ascends from left to right it shows ambition and aggressiveness. If the t bar is missing this indicates irresponsibility and carelessness.

$$l \;,\quad \underline{I} \;,\quad \iota \;,\quad \overset{o}{\iota}$$

A   B   C   D

$$\mathcal{T} \;,\quad T \;,\quad t \;,\quad \mathcal{I}$$

E   F   G   H

A = CLARITY & ASSURANCE   E = DEFINITE, EXTROVERT, PROTECTIVE
B = CONSTRUCTIVE THINKING   F = STRAIGHTFORWARD
C = ENTHUSIASTIC   G = AMBITIOUS
D = CREATIVE   H = ADVENTUROUS

The signature

Have you noticed how some people's signature bears no relationship whatsoever to their normal handwriting? Some have a very distinctive signature, others an unreadable scrawl. The signature is a very important aspect to consider when studying a sample because it is the image the person portrays to the outer world. When it bears little relationship to the normal handwriting you may find a divergence between the inner self and the outer image.

There are many factors to take into consideration when studying a person's signature. The name itself can have an important bearing on the way the owner makes her mark.

Generally speaking if the script for the first name is larger than that for the surname, the subject places more emphasis on personal abilities than on the family tradition. When the surname is larger than the forename, it means the subject is dominated by the family influence. If both names are in accord this shows a well-adjusted and self-confident person.

Ornate letters in a signature, especially in a forename, can show the need to be noticed; an unreadable signature can show the person's fear of 'being read'.

Is the signature underlined? This shows self-confidence, while a squiggle under the name is a sign of creativity. If the writer adds a full stop after the signature, this shows self-critical traits while an encircled signature, where the first letter surrounds the rest of the name, shows the need for cutting off from others, a need for aloneness.

How to interpret a sample

If you wish to interpret a sample of handwriting it might be best to analyse your own handwriting first. Look around for examples of your writing, from shopping lists to personal letters. Then take a good look at it and follow through each point in the following check-list:

Sample Check-list

Spacing	between words
	between lines
Originality	
Zones	upper
	middle
	lower
Slant	left
	vertical
	right
Size	
Regularity	
Pressure	
Connectedness	Connected
	Disconnected
Connections	
	arcade
	garland
	angular
	thready
Capitals	
Lead-ins	
Finals	
Capital l	
Small i	
Capital T	
Small t	
Signature	

How to find out more

Houston, AE, *Self-Analysis through Handwriting*, Coles Publishing Co Ltd, Canada, 1978.

Nezos, Renna, *Graphology*, Rider , 1989.

Olyanova, Nadya, *Handwriting Tells*, Wilshire Book Company, USA, 1969.

Singer Eric, *A Manual of Graphology*, Gerald Duckworth & Co, Treasure Press, England, 1987.

Aromatherapy

When you capture the aroma of a flower or shrub, do you feel your spirits lift? Does the scent of lavender calm you, the sharpness of lemongrass awaken your senses, the smell of mint work up your appetite? Does the aroma of a rose waft you back to the warm, sensuous days of mid-summer?

This is the magic of aromatherapy, the use of natural essential oils to relax and rejuvenate the tired body and spirit, a form of healing which has been in existence for thousands of years.

The philosophy of aromatherapy

Essential oils are given to us by nature. It is a small but essential part of the make-up of every plant, flower and shrub, that part which is known as its 'life force' or 'soul'. When we treat our bodies with these essential oils their power helps us to relax our nervous system, stimulate our circulatory process and rejuvenate our skin. They also help to re-balance the harmony between our mind and body, ease rheumatic pains, take away headaches and migraines and detoxify our entire body.

This life force which manifests itself in what we call essential oils is thought to be similar to our own hormones. It acts as a messenger of the entire plant, bringing together all the healing powers of that plant, including its aroma, to one place. It is this that is extracted from the plant and used in aromatherapy.

The goodness of these essences can be taken in through the nose or the mouth, but an aromatherapist will use massage to distribute the essences, for touch is considered to be integral in putting both the mind and the body into harmony with one another.

When used correctly, essential oils will not produce any side-effects; however in some cases when used in the wrong concentrations they can produce effects. All essences are both versatile and volatile, and can be mixed with each other to give different and in some cases, more effective, results.

Because of their volatile nature, essential oils can evaporate quickly and there are three specific classifications into which most essences fall: Top Note, Middle Note, Base Note.

The Top Note group which evaporate quickly are very fast-acting. These are used to uplift the spirit and invigorate the mind. The next is the Middle Note group which are not quite so quick to evaporate and are used for the stimulation and regulation of bodily functions such as metabolism, digestion and fertility cycles. The Base Note group are the slowest to evaporate and mixed with Top Note oils can regulate their evaporation. This group are used for relaxation and sedation purposes.

A short history of aromatherapy

Early records show that aromatherapy was used more than 4,000 years ago. The ancient Egyptians used aromatic essences for health of mind and body, for worshipping their gods and for casting magical spells. The age-old Egyptian mummies we now see still intact in museums have been treated with the embalming properties of cedarwood and sandalwood. In the nativity story, which is 2,000 years old, the magi presented the infant Jesus with gold, frankincense and myrrh, the first for wealth and the others for health in mind and body.

During the renaissance period the use of aromatic wines was popular for curing ailments such as burns, abrasions and for infected wounds.

The use of essential oils for health came back into practice during the First World War when aromatic ointments were used in both military and civilian hospitals. The essences would be put on to poultices, used in emulsions and in creams; it was discovered, or perhaps the word is 'rediscovered', that their properties greatly helped to accelerate healing. Skin absorbs the healing properties of these oils, and so for many years they have been added to ointments, salves and creams to aid in all sorts of ailments. Most essential oils act as antiseptics. In particular, lavender is especially effective in healing open wounds and burns, and also acts as a soporific, calming the mind in pain and helping the patient to sleep.

How aromatherapy works

Our sense of smell is much more powerful than we may think. It is linked to memory, to digestion, to sexual arousal. When our nose comes in contact with a scent an entire involuntary reaction occurs. Immediately, the scent travels up the olfactory nerve to the olfactory bulb just behind the bridge of the nose cavity. It then comes into contact with the cilia, tiny hairs which extend from nerve cells which in turn react to the scent, sending messages up the nerve cells back through the olfactory bulb and up to the brain. The message is received in the pituitary gland which controls our entire hormonal system. The message sent back could be a reaction of sexual arousal, hunger, stress, fear or memory.

Scents also travel into our lungs from the surrounding air we breathe. From our lungs they transfer to the blood and circulate in our blood-stream, carrying the effects of the scents to other parts of our body. Some scents, for instance lavender and orange blossom, are carried all around the body as they go to work on the skin. Others, such as rosemary, which works on liver problems, will have an affinity for one particular organ, so it will go there.

Healing properties within the essential oils move quickly through the skin and help increase the flow of blood supply to the tissues. In the case of oils such as lavender, sage, thyme and rosemary, these aid the cleaning action of the white corpuscles in the blood and in cell regeneration, and so encourage the rebuilding of damaged tissue. Such properties are particularly helpful in treating cancerous wounds.

The chemical explanation for the therapeutic effects of aromatherapy is as follows: we know that the pH shows the acidity or alkalinity of any solution. The weaker the pH value (which can vary from 0 - 14.14), the more acid the solution. In general, natural essences have an acid pH value. On the other hand, microbes of bacteria which cause illness thrive in alkalinity. A basic explanation of the powers of aromatherapy is, therefore, that the acid pH of a natural essence opposes such microbes and so wards them off.

Obtaining and using essential oils

Essential oils are usually extracted by distillation. Though called 'oils' they are often, in fact, quite watery to the touch and only a few drops are required in treatment. These drops are added to a 'carrier' such as coconut or grapeseed oil, in order to help its distribution over the necessary parts of the body in massage.

Should you buy your own essential oils you will find that there is quite a difference in price between certain essences. This is because different plants give different amounts of oil when extracted, and some plants are rarer than others, while some blossom for a short while and others for a much longer period. Also remember that although you will be charged a few pounds for a small bottle, only a few drops will be used for a therapy.

Although aromatherapy can be used in many ways, by inhaling, in massage, in the bath, in a compress, you will gain most in the hands of a fully-trained aromatherapist. However, if you wish to experiment, the following are some simple remedies which you may like to try. First, though, some important advice:

* Never put essences straight on to skin. They can burn. Always add to a 'carrier' first such as coconut, grapeseed or almond oil.

* Keep well away from the eyes. Should an essential oil get into your eye use a pure vegetable oil (ie sunflower, olive or almond oil) to flush it out. Do not use water!

* Although it is possible to add some essential oils to tea, etc. do not take any by drinking without the advice of a trained aromatherapist.

* Always replace the cap on the bottle of essential oil immediately after use as it evaporates quickly, and store out of sunlight in a dark bottle.

* Pregnant women should first seek advice from a trained aromatherapist before experimenting with any essences.

* Remember, only a few drops of essential oil are needed for any form of therapy.

Nature has provided us with many ways of treating our ailments and with sensible use of essential oils aromatherapy can cure many dis-eases in either mind or body.

Room refreshers
To refresh a room simply place a bowl of hot water in the room

114

and add a few drops of lavender or camomile essence.

Special candle holders are now available in which you place water and the essence of your choice. Then light the candle, and its gentle heat will warm the water which, in turn, transmits the required scent into your surroundings.

Put a little on a light bulb, and when the bulb heats up it will transmit the essence into the room. Do the same on a room radiator. When it warms up the essence will fill the room.

Inhalations

You can clear your lungs or air passages by using the oils in inhalations. All you need do is fill a bowl with boiling water and add the required essential oil. Lean over the bowl and place a towel over your head to trap the vapour. For a blocked nasal passage breathe in through your nose, and if you have a sore throat breathe in through your mouth. Essence of lavender should be used at nighttime to aid sleep, while eucalyptus or thyme should be used during the daytime.

Bathing

Aromatic baths are a very soothing and gentle way to benefit from the powers of aromatherapy. In this way the essences pass through the skin and are circulated in the blood-stream where they put their healing powers to work.

If you have difficulty in sleeping, add a few drops of lavender, lime flower or camomile to your bath. Lie back in the warm water and allow the essences to do the rest.

If you are a morning bather, add a few drops of rosemary (as an aid to concentration), sage or lemon grass to your bath water. This will help you waken up and keep your mind refreshed.

A bath with the added essence of bergamot is a good treatment for cystitis and for uplifting the spirits while the essences of rosemary, sage, basil and geranium are good for improving circulation and also for better muscular dynamics which would be of particular use to sports people. Add to the bath.

Other additives can be mint or anise for growth, while sandalwood, onion, cinnamon or norneal work as sexual stimulants. Camphor is good for calming sexual urges.

Skin problems from acne to eczema to psoriasis can be improved by many essential oils, including sandalwood, lavender, rosemary, bergamot, lemongrass and sage.

115

Compresses

When making a compress always use unmedicated lint or gauze or cotton wool.

If you suffer from menstrual cramp, make a hot compress by taking some clean cloth and putting it in hot water along with a few drops of marjoram oil. Wring out excess water and place this on the abdomen. When it cools, replenish it again and again until the cramps have subsided.

When suffering from sprains or bruises add a few drops of an analgesic oil such as lavender or camomile to hot or cold water. Soak the material in it for a few moments, then wring out excess water and apply repeatedly to the complaint.

Compresses are especially good for skin complaints and also for those suffering from rheumatic and arthritic problems.

Other tips

There are, of course, essences which can be used for anti-toxic and anti-venomous treatments, but should you be stung by an insect and have no essence handy, again nature has several cures which may be available to hand. Rub the flower of lavender or rosemary on to the sting, or cut into an onion or garlic clove and rub this on to the affected part. Within minutes the pain and the inflammation will disappear. In the case of a bee or wasp sting the sting should be removed by hand.

A few drops of lemon, rosemary or cedarwood added to a carrier oil and massaged into the scalp acts as a wonderful hair conditioner and is very good for dry scalp.

Essence of clove is very good for toothache and, when used regularly, can heal an abscess.

Coughing at night? Then sprinkle a few drops of cypress oil on your pillow before going to bed.

If you simply cannot stop hiccuping then put a couple of drops of essence of tarragon on your tongue and they will cease.

What aromatherapy massage can do for you

Aromatherapy is a very enjoyable way to alleviate problems whether physical or psychological. Surrounded by the wonderful aromas provided in abundance by nature, the skilled aromatherapist can revitalise you in mind and body, using a combination of healing essential oils and the therapeutic method of massage.

To benefit from an aromatherapy session you don't have to

wait until you fall ill. Indeed treatment with essential oils will improve your energy levels, make you sleep better, will make you feel in better health both mentally and physically, while helping to ward off such illness as flu and colds.

The skilled aromatherapist can use her own massage techniques together with the techniques of reflexology or massage on the pressure points recognised by Shiatsu.

An aromatherapist usually combines the required essence with massage, which in itself is revitalising. Following the blood and lymph pressure flow, stress and relaxation points, the therapist will use different massage techniques in order to enhance well-being in mind and body.

The following is a short list of just some of the complaints which can be treated by an aromatherapist:

When aromatic essences are used for cuts and abrasions, healing occurs quickly and without any dangers of toxicity or the formation of scars. It can be used to actually rid the skin of old scars too.

Colitis can be treated by lavender, sage, rosemary and thyme, and these essences can also be used to detoxify the entire body. *Intestinal infections* can be cured by garlic, onion, anise, lemon, juniper and thyme.

Problems with the *menstrual cycle* can be treated with such essences as rue, valerian, basil, cinnamon, mint, cumin, lavender and thyme.

Breast-feeding mothers may be interested to know that essence of anise, caraway, fennel and lemongrass increase lactation, while parsley, mint and sage reduce it.

Juniper works as an antiseptic and as a cleanser, and can help in the problems of *water retention, obesity* and for *clearing the mind* of worrying thoughts.

Arterial complaints can be treated with essence of lavender, aspic or marjoram to lower blood pressure, while hyssop, rosemary, sage and thyme can raise it.

Diabetes can be helped with the anti-diabetic properties of eucalyptus, onion or geranium.

An aromatherapy session

Aromatherapy is another holistic form of treatment where the entire individual and her way of life is taken into account by the therapist. When attending an aromatherapist make sure you give any personal or medical history which might be relevant. You will find that a session is highly personalised and your aromatherapist will not only give you a massage using essential oils but will also cover advice on future diet, way of life and will take emotional factors into consideration.

Before attending an aromatherapist do not take alcohol or have a full meal. It will also be a help to you both if you arrive in a relaxed manner rather than tense; the treatment will work more quickly on a relaxed mind and body. Also, try to schedule the time following the treatment so that you don't immediately have to rush off and build up tension again. You should not take a shower or bath for at least six hours after the session, in order to allow the beneficial properties of the oils to take full effect.

After the initial diagnostic discussion the therapist will mix whatever essences are required with a natural vegetable oil which acts as a 'carrier' to spread the essences over and into the skin. The essences may also be added to creams or lotions and applied locally to a specific area, or massaged all over the body. If you find it difficult to take all your clothes off for the massage at the initial session do tell the therapist and then you need only take off the clothes you feel comfortable about.

You will find that the massage is soothing, because the philosophy of aromatherapy takes into account both your mental and physical state, unlike the Swedish-type massage where only the physical make-up is taken into consideration.

How to find out more

Davis, Patricia, *Aromatherapy, an A-Z*, CW Daniel & Company, Englnad, 1988.
Price, Shirley, *Practical Aromatherapy*, Thorsons, England, 1987.
Worwood, Valerie Ann, *The Fragrant Pharmacy*, Macmillan, London, 1990.
Martin, Gill, *Alternative Health, Aromatherapy*, Optima, England, 1989.

Palmistry

Our hands are an important tool for communication: just look at how we 'speak' with our hands when we cannot communicate verbally. When we want to get an important point across we use not only words but also our hands. When we care for someone we show it by touch. And when we shake hands on meeting so much can be given away by that hand-shake. Is it firm and confident, or does it resemble the touch of a wet fish? Is the full hand extended or are just the tips of the fingers offered and the rest of the hand held back? Quite often we let our intuition take over and tell us whether we like a person from the moment our hands touch. How often our first impressions prove to be correct!

There is a way to discover at a glance the hidden motivations which impel each of us through life, and it is the study of the secrets of the hand. This is a blend of intuitive talent and the science of palmistry and it can immediately tell you all you need to know about the character and motivations of friends, foes and colleagues.

How palmistry works

Palmistry is more than just the study of the lines on the palm of the hand (known as chiromancy). It also requires the study of the shape of the hand (chirognomy), and the study of the skin patterns of the fingers and the palm's surface (dermatoglyphics). By studying palmistry you can read a person's past, present and future as though it were a map spread out in front of you.

No two hands are the same, not even your own! While the overall shape of the hand and fingers does not change, the lines do; it is thought that palm lines reflect the energy channels in a person's life and so they change as that person's life changes.

In a right-handed person the right hand is the dominant and

the left is the non-dominant. The opposite applies for a left-handed person. The non-dominant hand is said to show what you are born with, and the dominant hand shows what you do with that set of circumstances, traits and talents. A comparison between the dominant and non-dominant hand shows a fascinating history of how the person has adapted to changing circumstances and can show how a change thrust upon the person has been overcome by will-power and determination to survive. This can be especially evident when a person's palm print is taken this year, then another taken two to three years later. Depending on changing circumstances and attitudes, differences will be easy to see; sometimes a totally new life line can show, or perhaps the heart line can appear more strong and positive. It is also interesting where possible to study palm prints before and after a traumatic change in a person's life.

No single feature will be taken into account when a reading is undertaken, rather each significant fact will be assessed in an overall view. Both the left hand (in the right-handed person the non-dominant or inherited hand) and the right (the dominant or the achievement hand) should be read together. In this way it is possible to see what the person has done with the abilities she or he was born with, as well as present behaviour and energy and how this is being channelled.

A short history of palmistry

Palmistry appears to have been developed in India before the *Vedas* (the four holy books Hinduism) were written, while some say the first traces of palmistry date back to the third century BC in China. Wherever and whenever palmistry originated it is believed that Greek and Arab traders brought it to Europe and in more recent times it has become a trade of the travelling gipsies.

There is little written evidence of palmistry before the thirteenth century AD, but this is possibly because it was taught by word of mouth rather than in written form. One of the earliest written records is known as *The Digby Roll IV*, a manuscript on palmistry written in Middle English, around 1440 AD, which mentions the importance of the life, head, heart and fate lines, the influence of the planets and certain other marks.

Palmistry has always been more popular in Continental

Europe. During the Elizabethan period an Italian, Barthelmy Cocles was a noted palmist and even predicted the date and manner of his own death. He also used palmistry to diagnose medical illness. Paracelsus, the founder of medical chemistry who lived in the early sixteenth century, was a well-respected palmist and made numerous references to it in his works.

As the rational sciences became more pronounced in the seventeenth and eighteenth centuries, the study of the physical overtook that of the psychical and so interest in such sciences as palmistry and astrology waned. However, the study of hand shapes and their relationship to psychological traits was developed and became the recognised science of chirognomy. It was Count Louis Harmon, otherwise known as Cheiro, who brought palmistry back into popularity in the twentieth century with his natural charm and charisma. He advised such personages as Dame Nellie Melba, Mark Twain and Sarah Bernhardt and in this way, palmistry once more became acceptable in society.

Taking a handprint

The simplest way to develop a talent at palmistry is to begin by studying your own handprints. This will give you insight into your behaviour and also, if you keep samples of your prints over the years you will be able to study how your energy has taken you down different paths in personal relationships and in your career. You might then begin to study your friends' handprints, but always remember that whatever you say will be taken seriously, so think first before making a sweeping statement which could affect the person's future. Also, remember it is essential to read both handprints for the dominant and non-dominant in order to give a true reading.

Simple handprints can be made by placing the hand palm-downwards on an inked rubber stamp pad or by using the contents of a paint-box, then pressing the hand on to a sheet of paper. However, this will only give you a basic map of the hand and a full study would not be easy under these circumstances.

If you are seriously going to study a hand-print you will need to make very close examination of all its elements, so get the type of magnifying eye-piece that a stamp-collector would use, together with a metric ruler, a notepad and pen.

To take a good handprint you will need the following: a sheet of glass, a sheet of white A4 typing paper (with no water mark), a tube of water-based ink so that it can be washed off easily afterwards, a roller of some sort to distribute the ink and a wide implement similar to a rolling pin to ensure an even spread of the hand on the paper.

Squeeze 2 inches of ink on to the sheet of glass and roll it out until it is evenly distributed. Ask the person to put the first hand on to the ink and ensure that the full hand, fingers and wrist are inked. Now put the sheet of paper over the rolling pin with the edge of the paper close to the person's hand, and the rolling pin at the top edge. Place the hand on to the paper, then using the rolling pin underneath, roll under the hand from the fingertips to the top of the wrist. In this way you can be sure that the full inked hand print is recorded on the paper. Take the paper away from the top end as the hand is lifted upwards from the paper. Now do the same with the other hand without re-inking the glass sheet.

To clean the inked hand, run under a flowing cold tap first, then use warm water and soap.

When the ink has dried on the sheet put some sort of mark on the back to act as a reference for the future, eg name, date, left or right hand print and which is the dominant hand.

Remember when reading a print that it is like looking at a mirror reflection; in other words when the thumb is shown on the left-hand side of the page then it is the print of a right-hand.

How to read a handprint

It is a good idea to keep a notepad handy and jot down the basic facts you discover about each handprint. A quick, useful 'checklist' is shown at the end of this section.

Before going into an analysis of a handprint it is vitally important that you remember to inquire whether the person is right or left-handed so that you read the dominant and non-dominant hand correctly.

The shape of the hand
First of all the shape of the hand can tell a lot about a personality. To get a true reading look at the palm side, not the back, as these can give two totally different views. According to Casimir

d'Arpentigny, who was a devotee of palmistry in the nineteenth century, and whose beliefs are still advocated today, there are seven types of hand, as follows:

Square: Here the lower palm is squarely set on to the wrist with equal width at the base of the fingers and the base of the palm. The overall impression is one of solidity. The square hand can show reliability, patience and method. However, it can also show a 'square' attitude, with stubborn views and resistance to change.

Conic: The base of the fingers and the base of the palm are slightly tapering, with rounded fingertips clearly defined, giving an overall impression of roundedness. Conic hands are also known as artistic, and they denote creativity, versatility and impulsiveness. These people are fast-moving and often yearn for change for the sake of change.

Spatulate: The base at the wrist is broader than the base of the fingers, or vice versa, and there are broad fingertips. The personality is independent, creative and very energetic. Where there is a wider base at the fingers it denotes an active mind, while a wider base at the palm end indicates an active body.

Psychic: The entire hand and fingers are long and narrow, with tapered fingertips. The idealistic owners of these hands are not of this world. They are too trusting and allow their energy to flow out of their long finger tips indiscriminately, losing their power and being easily influenced by lack of judgement.

Philosophic: This hand is long, bony and has distinctly knotted finger joints, with lengthy nail phalanges. People with such hands tend to be too busy untangling the knotty problems of the universe and the deeper questions of the psyche to take time for the mundane matters of life. They are proud, aesthetic and sensitive.

Elementary: In contrast to the intellectually-inclined philosophic hand, the elementary hand is short in length and wide in breadth. These are the hands of the physical worker who is more close to the earth than the heavens. Allowing the instinct to take command, this personality is a sound character who has no interest in the artificial.

Mixed: This is the category into which most people fall. While it is somewhat difficult to determine, the mixed hand can contain a spatulate palm with one or more long, tapering finger, and the others knotty, or otherwise. Mixed hand personalities find it easy to adapt to change and are always open to new ventures and ideas.

The shape of the fingers

The length of the fingers in proportion to the palm can be found by measuring the middle finger from its lowest point to its tip, then comparing this to the measurement of the palm from the 'bracelet' at the wrist to the bottom of the middle finger. If the finger is longer than the palm then the person has long fingers; if it is shorter then the person is considered to have short fingers.

Those with short fingers are quick-thinking, adaptable people who are the initiators of innovative projects but who rarely have the patience to see them through to the end. They should work with those with long fingers who are slower thinkers but are happy to attend to detail and work methodically to achieve the end result.

When studying the fingers, take note of the length of each phalange, the three sections into which each finger is divided. The phalange at the finger tip is the 1st phalange, the one beneath is the 2nd and the phalange nearest the palm is the 3rd. Just as every part of the body is related to a planet or a star, astrology and mythology are also brought to bear in palmistry. The following is a brief outline of how different parts of the hand are related in some way to either or both:

The *first finger* is called after Jupiter, the king of the gods who stands for justice, leadership, career and financial ambition, and represents the individual's willpower over others. Note how, when we want to warn someone of their behaviour, for instance, we wag our first finger at them to get our verbal point across.

The *middle finger* is named after Saturn, the introspective god who searches for truth in scientific and metaphysical studies. This represents the knowledge of right and wrong. Watch out if you see a short Saturn finger!

The *'ring' finger* is named after Apollo, the god who rules over creativity and artistry. Apollo is associated with the love of beauty and the ability for self-expression. A long Apollo finger indicates a great love of self-expression.

The *'little' finger* is named after Mercury, the quick-witted, fast-talking, and speedy messenger of the gods. Mercury represents communication at all levels, successful commerce and the power of speech. A long Mercury finger shows a talent for diplomacy.

The *thumb* symbolises the person's will, and therefore is not apportioned a god. The thumb rises from the Mount of Venus, the goddess of love, sexuality and sensuality. In India an entire reading would be based on the thumb only, and if you wish to get a fast, basic key to a person's character, take a look at the thumb. Again, the dominant and non-dominant hand will often show differing thumbs. The thumb can be divided into will-power (1st phalange), and logic (2nd phalange). If the thumb is stiff it shows an inflexible attitude towards others, and if supple, impulsiveness.

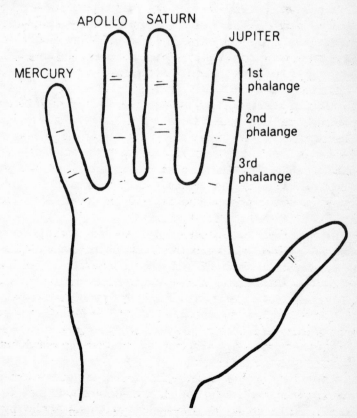

The mounts

The mounts are storehouses of energy relating to each part of the hand which they represent. There are eight mounts on each palm, and the first four are directly under the fingers. The Jupiter mount is a storehouse of energy for the Jupiter finger, the Saturn mount is the same for the Saturn finger and so on. When the mounts are fully formed this means they are full of energy for that particular purpose. For instance, a full Apollo mount would represent a desire to express oneself in the arts in some way. A full Mercury mount would be bursting with energy to express oneself in communication of some sort, through writing, in the media, in politics, perhaps.

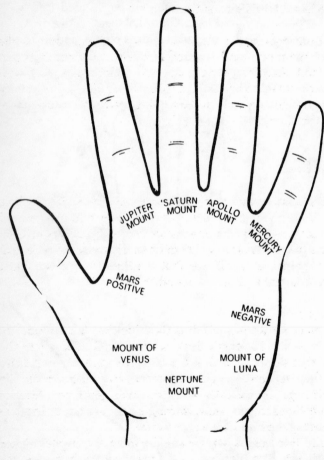

The remaining mounts are found lower in the palm. There are two Mars mounts, the Upper Mars and the Lower Mars. Upper Mars is found just below the Mercury mount. This shows the level of quiet perseverance in a person who may seem very easy-going until coming up against opposition. Then watch out! The Lower mount is found between the head line and the thumb. This also denotes resistance, but an open resistance in this case. The mount of Venus runs from the base of the thumb to the life line and denotes basic emotions from love of family to love of life and sexuality. A fully-developed Venus mount shows a great physical vitality especially in regard to sexuality and sensuality. It also shows a basic generosity towards others, and a warm welcome to visitors and strangers.

The Luna mount, on the opposite side of the palm, is the mount of the moon, and is associated with tidal comings and goings (and therefore travel), as well as things to do with philosophy, imagination and mysticism. A full Luna mount shows a good imagination and a leaning towards learning more through travel or gaining knowledge.

The main lines

Most people know that there are three main lines, the life line, the head line and the heart line. There is usually a fourth line, the fate line, although this is not seen on everyone's hands. It is on these lines that the major aspects of one's life are shown. Look at your two palms. You will see that the lines on the dominant palm are different to those on the other.

The life line
Almost everyone knows which is their life line, but contrary to what is believed, its length does not necessarily show you the length of that person's life; it is more likely to show the intensity of their life. Depending on circumstances and attitudes the life line can change dramatically when someone 'gets a new lease of life' by meeting someone new, starting a new project, or in some way changing their outlook on the future.

The life line begins somewhere between the Jupiter finger and the thumb. The higher on the Jupiter mount it begins, the more ambitious that person will be, a clear leader, and when it starts on the Lower Mars mount it shows the person to be more passive. Most people's life line starts at a mid-point between the two.

The best way to guess at the chronological order of events is to assume the beginning of the life line at age 1, and the base of the life line at, say, age 65-70. Draw an imaginary line half-way between the two and you get age 30-35.

When the life line and the head line share the same beginning, it means a close-knit family relationship which might prove dependent until the head line breaks away.

The following is a brief outline of personality traits shown in the life line:

Long/deep: this shows a realistic attitude to life unencumbered by health worries or heartaches.
Short/deep: this shows an intensity of living, with possible recklessness.
Short/weak: this person is a passive, introverted personality.

If the life line ends on the Luna mount it denotes a restlessness and need for travel. When there are branches off the life line towards the Luna mount this shows a journey - long if the branch is long, short if it is short. If the line moves towards the Luna mount but ends on the Venus mount the person will enjoy travelling but will prefer to end up at home.

When the life line hugs the thumb it shows a timid, domesticated personality.

Sometimes you may find another line branching off towards the thumb. This is known as the 'inner life line' or the 'line of Mars', and shows added strength and physical or spiritual vitality.

The head line
The head line shows the intellectual capacity and workings of the personality you are analysing. The shape, whether it runs straight across, curves deeply or joins another line, denotes the analytical or imaginative potential; the form of the head line, which can be deep, faint or chained, shows the ability to think clearly and the quality of memory, while the length of the line shows the flexibility of that mental attitude.

Like the life line, the source of the head line can begin

anywhere from the mount of Jupiter to the mount of lower Mars. The higher it begins the higher the intellect and more honourable the person, the lower the line the more cautious and less intellectual. Often the life line and the head line begin together, which means a family tie which usually breaks away after the early years.

If the head line and the life line are wide apart this can mean impetuosity and rash decision-making, while a narrow space shows independence and good self-motivation.

The line itself, when it shows clear and deep, is the sign of a clear thinker. If it is faint or chained the person might have problems following through to a conclusion, while a wavering line means a wavering mind, unable to make a decision.

A short head line shows concentration on one purpose, with little interest in overall knowledge. In contrast a long line which runs straight across the palm shows a person who is interested in the truth but is somewhat fixed in mind and has a cold, analytical nature.

The line that bends slightly towards the Luna mount shows a versatile imagination, while a sharp angle towards the same mount shows an imagination which, if running uncontrolled, can cause psychological problems. When the head line forks in two this shows a talent for using intellect to see both sides of a situation. The head line which runs almost parallel to the life line is the sign of creative energy which, if correctly channelled, can show a great composer or writer.

The heart line
The heart line or line of emotion shows the person's attitudes to love and intimacy. While the relationship line is shown elsewhere, the heart line can show attitudes towards love and involvement.

Unlike the head and life lines, this originates from the area of the mount of Mercury, and if the beginning of this line is chained it shows an early insecurity, while if it is strong it denotes knowledge of love and succour.

A clear, deep line shows a secure, loving person, while a weak or chained line shows insecurity in love. If the line shows strongly on the palm and divides into three branches at the end it shows a loving, committed attitude in three differing roles, ie in a family situation, towards the world at large and in a personal sexual relationship.

If the heart line is close to the base of the fingers, this can mean a sensitive person who tends to be subjective in personal relationships. If the heart line runs closer to the head line this means the 'head rules the heart'.

The heart line can extend all the way across the palm, which shows a willingness to become everyone's friend, yet give oneself wholly to no one person. If it stops and starts again it can mean a change of attitude towards involvement, and if it runs all the way up to the mount of Saturn this shows a search for the ideal partner. The heart line ending in the Jupiter mount shows a person who is passionate and possessive in love, while if it runs between Jupiter and Saturn mounts it shows a realistic, mature attitude towards relationships.

The fate line

The fate line shows the pathway to achievement, indicating personal drive and ambition. This line begins at the base of the palm, and travels upwards towards the base of the fingers. Not everyone has a fate line, and while this means there is no inner call to a true path in life, it does not mean that nothing will be achieved.

If the fate line originates from the life line, this indicates an independent entrepreneurial spirit, and that success will be achieved through one's own efforts. When the line begins nearer the head line, this means a successful career will be found later in life. The palm with the line coming from between the mounts of Venus and Luna shows success from a balance between personal commitment and help from others.

When the fate line leans into the mount of Luna it shows a career dealing with others. It also indicates that success will depend on other people's help. A line extending deep into Luna and almost to the edge of the palm shows a deep commitment to the psychic arts and healing.

When the fate line ends between Saturn and Apollo this shows a tendency towards technical artistry such as that in architecture, graphic design and recording engineers. The fate line ending deep in the mount of Jupiter shows in the hand of someone in the public eye, while one ending in the Saturn mount means security and success throughout life.

The relationship and children line

These lines are found at the side of the palm on the Mercury mount area, near the heart line. As in all palmistry, these lines denote potential relationship or children rather than certainty.

The relationship lines show stable relationships, and are short and run horizontally at the side of the palm. Your print may show three deep horizontal lines but you may have had only one lasting relationship and have no intention or necessity to have any more. From these horizontal lines you can sometimes find vertical lines running upwards. These show the potential for children.

As these are potential situations, you can often find some people who are in relationships and have three children having no relationship or children lines, while others with both horizontal and vertical lines showing may be single and childless.

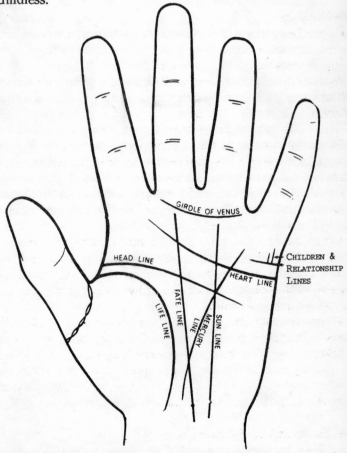

Other marks

As you will find when you study a palm print, there are many other marks to be found on individual palms. A basic explanation is: *Stars* and *crosses* mean sudden changes which could be for good or bad. *Islands* and chains mean obstacles occurring, while *squares* show positive events. *Grilles* show temporary problems which can be overcome, and *triangles* show good luck and positive energy.

Where these marks fall on the hands will show the areas of life they will affect.

Before reading a palm

Before undertaking a reading of anyone's palms, including your own, keep foremost in your mind the awareness that palmistry foretells what is probable, not what is certain. The person's future can be changed by a change in attitude or direction, and so what you read in the palm today can change radically over months or years.

There is such a science as medical palmistry, where specialists in palmistry can diagnose certain illness through markings on the palm. This, however, is for the expert only.

When giving a reading, bear in mind that no matter how nonchalant the person appears to be, your comments will be taken seriously and could have a lasting effect on that person's beliefs and future attitudes. As you gain experience you will be able to use your intuition more together with your knowledge of the basics of palmistry, and know how deeply you can go in a reading.

CHECK-LIST

Name: **Date:**

Hand shape
Square
Conic
Spatulate
Psychic
Philosophic
Elementary
Mixed

Shape of fingers
Jupiter finger
Saturn finger
Apollo finger
Mercury finger
The thumb

The mounts
Luna
Lower Mars
Jupiter
Saturn
Apollo
Mercury
Upper Mars
Venus

The lines
Life line
Head line
Heart line
Fate line
Relationship line
Children lines

Other Marks

How to find out more

Altma Nathanie, *The Art of Psychological Hand Analysis*, Aquarian Press, England, 1984.
Reid Lori, *How to Read Hands*, Aquarian Press, England, 1984.
Gittelson Bernard, *Intangible Evidence*, Positive Paperbacks, Simon & Schuster, London, 1989.

Self-Healing Through Imaging

Although we are all alive, how many of us are truly living? Why are some people so successful in friendships, in careers, in business matters? Why do some people never need to enter a hospital, while others spend so many precious days and months suffering one or another form of dis-ease? How come some people get close to achieving success yet hold back at the last moment, while others succeed as though by some unspoken right? Is success achieved through aptitude or attitude?

The secret of success is, in fact, the amalgamation of both aptitude and attitude. Any achievement is possible once you recognise your own aptitude and correctly focus your attitude to succeed by using this aptitude to the full.

Recognising your aptitude means that if you want to work in broadcasting but your voice does not come over well you don't throw in the towel. Look at what you are good at - perhaps organisation - and train as a producer, instead, or if you are good at putting words together become a scriptwriter. It just needs a change in attitude. In matters of success in wealth or health you can be a 'hopeful case' or a 'hopeless case'. The choice is yours. You can achieve your choice through imaging. If you are to succeed in this it is imperative that you do not confuse 'imaging' with 'wishing thinking'. The two are poles apart. Imaging is where you discard the old image of yourself ('I am a smoker,' 'I am always getting colds,' 'I am always being over-looked in promotion ...') and re-programming your mind with a new image of yourself: ('If I am no longer a smoker,' 'I am always well,' etc). To do this you must re-programme your sub-conscious when in a relaxed state.

Your mind is your most powerful possession. Used positively it can be your greatest ally. Used negatively it can prove to be your deadliest enemy. Using the full potential of your mind can put you on the right path to attain your aspirations in health, wealth and personal relationships.

It is generally held that only 10 per cent of the brain is used by most individuals. That means there is an enormous 90 per cent of unused brain power waiting to be utilised. Who knows what each of us could achieve if we learned to tap into this powerful resource of innate potential!

The power of the psyche

The brain is like an iceberg. Only the very tip is seen and used. This is the ego or the conscious self. The vast remainder of the mind - the psyche - is hidden. (The psyche is also known as the id or the sub-conscious.) Because we cannot see it and because we cannot measure it in scientific terms the power of our sub-conscious is usually ignored and rarely encouraged. Yet it is this hidden power which guides us in all that we do in our career, our lifestyle, our relationships.

Up until now you may have been happy enough to let life jog along, on occasion allowing yourself to be pulled hither and thither by your sub-conscious actions, feeling out of control of your future. Yet it doesn't have to be that way because you can decide on the pathway you choose to follow through your life. You can control your life. The way to do this is by re-training your sub-conscious to follow a different pathway in the future by the method of creative visualisation and imaging.

How the mind works

To understand how imaging works, we first have to understand how the mind works. The brain is made up of two sides - the left and right hemispheres.

The left hemisphere looks after essentially the logical aspect of our lives: our reasoning abilities, the 'three R's' (reading, writing and arithmetic), our analytical aptitude and our language skills.

The Right hemisphere is concerned with our emotions, our powers of imagination, our dreams, our visual recognition and our sense of rhythm.

As pre-school children we use both parts of the brain. We experiment in language, in reasoning, in visual ability, in rhythm, and our imaginations are unbounded. However, we then enter the classroom and here we are taught to concentrate on the growth of the left-hand side of the brain. If you want to find out how much money you will have left at the end of the month you will use the left-hand side of your brain to work out the answer. If you want to remember how a scene from a play went or the design of last year's fashions you will use the right-hand side of your brain. The talents of the right hemisphere of the brain are usually channelled into out-of-school hobbies, perhaps ignored or sometimes even quashed.

If we are lucky we might fall, often by accident, into a career which allows us to be our real selves and encourages us to fulfil our true potential. This is quite a unusual, however. Most people who make their career out of their creative abilities, be they artists, writers, media personalities, have usually come to their success through many a past 'failure', their lives being termed a 'failure' by non-creative peers and elders who are nervous of their creative imagination. How many people do you know who live lives of 'quiet desperation', locked into unfulfilling careers for thirty or forty years? It is no wonder so many people's minds and bodies stop working effectively under such circumstances.

While all this emphasis is placed on developing our brain's left hemisphere, the right side, our centre of creativity, is being overlooked. Yet it is this side which creates the images on which we base our behaviour. It is here that we conjure up images of our future, images of what gives us pleasures, what moves or touches us. These are images which can be seen, heard, felt, tasted, smelled.

Even if our left hemisphere has trained us to be the best scientist or the best multi-lingual correspondent, if our right hemisphere is seeing a low self-image we will never accept or fulfil our true potential. To be fulfilled in whatever role we choose for ourselves we must have our left and right hemispheres working in balance and harmony, so that we can have a true self-image of.

The importance of self-image
In certain important ways, you are what you think you are. Close your eyes for a moment and think of your physical image. Do you feel you are too fat, too thin, out of proportion, ugly, attractive? Is your hair a flowing mane, a tangled web? Is your smile a grimace or does it brighten others' lives? In reality you are most likely a perfectly interesting person with traits which other people admire. Yet because of a low self-image you feel

you are unworthy of admiration.

Self-image is a self-fulfilling prophecy. This is a fact. Our sub-conscious acts not in accordance with reality, but in accordance with our perception of reality. Our sub-conscious cannot tell the difference between a real event and one that is vividly imagined again and again. This is good news, because it in effect means that if we tell our sub-conscious something, and keep repeating it, it will accept it as a fact and act accordingly. You will no longer accept situations in which you are not happy. If you are in an unhappy relationship you will do something to change it, for you no longer see your image as fitting the situation. If you are 'trapped' in a bad job, you will no longer remain in that trap. Your sub-conscious image shows a different 'you' and will put you on the road to achieving it. This might mean improving your qualifications through study, it many mean learning a new skill, it may mean taking a cut in salary to move jobs. Socially you may change your unhappy environment by speaking out, by protesting, by becoming political. Instead of imagining yourself a failure at a job interview, for example, imagine yourself as a success. Imagine yourself as showing your very best, positive charming characteristics and this is exactly what you will do.

To succeed with imaging there is one very important point that you must keep uppermost in your thoughts: *you are in charge of your own mind* - both conscious and sub-conscious - at all times. *No one can think any thought in your mind but you*. Outsiders may try to, and often fool you into accepting their thoughts. But now that you know you are in charge of your mind all those old low-image beliefs can change and stay where they belong, in the past. You no longer have to accept what other people say as the only truth. What you believe is true. This is why self-image is a self-fulfilling prophecy.

It is just as easy to accept good thoughts as it is to accept bad thoughts. Most of us have been trained since our earliest days to accept negative thoughts. Our siblings might have said we were ugly, and we found that easy to accept. Our teachers said we were foolish, and we never questioned their opinions. Our parents or partners made us feel unlovable, and we found no problem telling ourselves they were right. So with all this experience behind us, we have probably had plenty of practice accepting negative thoughts without ever querying them.

It is again our self-image which motivates us in the matter of material gain and success in personal relationships. If we see ourselves as always counting pennies, always 'making do', always 'just getting by', then this prophecy will be fulfilled. We shall never have any personal financial wealth. Whenever we receive a financial bonus we shall be faced with an unexpected financial outlay. So again we shall be 'just getting by'. The same applies to personal relationships. If we always see ourselves as meeting worthless prospective partners, those are the types we shall meet. If we have been disappointed in the past it is easy to feel we shall be disappointed in the future. And, again, this prophecy will be fulfilled.

To change our circumstances we have to change our attitude and in this way we can realise our true self. We do this by re-training our sub-conscious with imaging.

First steps in positive imaging

From this moment, however, we no longer have to accept negative thoughts. From this moment we can accept only positive thoughts. Dump negative beliefs from your mind now! Try this exercise: Get a notepad and write down all those negative beliefs you have been holding for years. 'I'm so unlovable no one could ever love me.' 'I'm so stupid I'll always be a failure' etc. etc. Now find a pen with a big nib and made a bold cross all the way through those negative beliefs. Keep crossing the words out until you can no longer see them. They are your enemies and they shouldn't be allowed to exist!

Now those old, negative images no longer exist, so your old, negative thoughts can no longer exist. Do you feel suddenly free?

Remember you are in charge of all the thoughts that enter your mind. Don't allow a negative thought in for a second. Think of your mind as an empty room with a door. Think of positive thoughts as being like bright, shining stars, and negative thoughts like the hidden part of the moon, dark and threatening.

You are now standing within your mind-room, holding the key to the locked door in your hand. You are alone and at peace. Then you hear a knock on the door. It is a dark, negative thought trying to come in, but remember the door is locked against it and you hold the key to the door. Every time a dark, negative thought tries to enter your mind-room you can close the door firmly in its face and lock it. Build up a barricade to keep it out if you have to. Imagine yourself like a sentry at that door, hammering nails into planks of wood to keep that door shut at all times against those negative thoughts. Take down that barricade and open the door only when a bright shining positive thought knocks for entry.

You can see it is a positive thought because it shines so brightly, just like a star. The negative thoughts hate the light so they back off and hide in the shadows. Soon you won't have to worry about letting them into your mind-room because they know there's no room for them there; all the space has been taken by those bright shining positive thoughts.

Wouldn't the world be a much better place if we all loved one another instead of living in fear and hostility? Yet we cannot love others until we love ourselves. We must learn to love ourselves first; not love ourselves above others in a selfish way, but love ourselves because of others. Then when we love ourselves we can give out some of that love to others, not for personal gain but out of genuine care.

Now look in a mirror, and say out loud 'I am a beautiful sight to behold.' Say 'I have a beautiful body.' Say 'I am so lovable that everyone loves me'. Keep telling yourself how good you are. This is not a practice of indulgent pride, but a lesson in self-love.

Practise positive thoughts all the time. Move into a positive consciousness. When you are walking down the street you are constantly in touch with and being influenced by, events and people around you. Think of the air through which you pass as being made up of positive (pink) energy bubbles, and negative (navy blue) bubbles. As you move along, allow your body to be surrounded only by the pink bubbles. Shrug off the navy blue negative bubbles.

When you are in the company of someone who constantly gripes and moans about the world, the weather, the future, and so on, don't let this negativity affect you. Keep it away by crossing your feet and holding your hands together. You are closing your extremities off from negative influence.

Now that you see how you can influence your own belief patterns it is easy to understand how whatever you believe can become reality for you. Instead of believing negative things you can change your life in important ways by changing your attitude and believing only the positive things. With the right attitude, there is much in our lives that we can actively change.

Students at medical colleges are told that the mind and body are distinctly separate. They are taught how to heal the body only. To discover how to heal the mind, these students would then have to undertake a further course in psychology. This means that neither medical nor psychology students are taught to treat both mind and body as an integral whole.

Yet the mind and the body are not separate. The mind cannot function without the nourishment it receives from the body in blood and oxygen. The body cannot function without the messages it receives from the brain.

To understand the importance of the balance of harmony in the mind, we must remember that we all originate from just one embryo. As the embryo grows within the womb it divides into three distinct functions: the first is the brain, the second the hormonal system, the third the nervous system.

The brain controls the pituitary gland which is a small ductless gland at the base of the brain. The pituitary gland creates hormones, from the Greek word for 'messenger'. The 'messengers' send signals down to the rest of the body and tell the nervous system how to react in a given situation.

If for some reason the brain is out of harmony, it becomes muddled and sends confused messages to the hormones. These, in turn, send muddled messages to the nervous system. The result can be all sorts of dis-ease of both the mind and the body. Skin disorders, organ and limb malfunction, are all caused by the brain being in a confused state.

The workings of the brain can be likened to a computer system. The memory bank of a computer (the brain) commands the program software (the hormones) which in turn command the computer hardware (the nervous system). Let's imagine that a town planner needs to forecast the requirements for second level education in your area. New information on population movement in the district will be put into the computer which will then be asked to calculate future needs, and will be collected on the final print-out. Everything works in harmony. Information is put into the computer memory. The memory makes calculations. The calculations are sent to the printer. However, during the calculations an electrical fault occurs. The memory bank gets confused. It sends confused messages to the software. The software sends confused messages to the printer.

141

The printer types out information which makes no sense. You do not, however, waste time trying to mend the printer; instead you look for the fault within the computer memory, where it occurred.

From such an example it is easy to understand why we sometimes suffer from dis-ease of our body (the soma) when we are living in some form of dis-harmony in our mind (the psyche). When the medical profession say, therefore, that most illnesses are 'psychosomatic' they are making an accurate diagnosis, because this means 'mind over body'. Regrettably, such a diagnosis is too often used dismissively as though the patient is 'imagining' the problem and that the problem only exists in the brain. The fact, however, is that the problem exists because of the brain; it is a mind-over-body disfunction.

However, because today's medical profession have been taught that mind and body are separate, they tend to skate over the psychosomatic condition and treat dis-ease as though it has been brought about by an outside agent. So the real issue underlying the complaint - the disharmony in the mind - is ignored.

When the brain is out of harmony due to lack of love, lack of exercise, lack of nutrition, lack of relaxation, it will send out signals for help in the form of dis-ease. These signals can be in any form, for instance psoriasis, eczema, arthritis, heart-attack, cancerous growth, insomnia, ulceration, flu, fatigue and so on. If we listen to our body we can hear its messages.

To cure these dis-eases, instead of operating on the outside, a change is needed from within. A change in outlook, in diet, in lifestyle. Every person has the ability to effect an inner cure, for the dis-ease which is created from within can be treated by a healer from within, the mind's sub-conscious. What is required is a willing attitude towards change.

As Dr Bernie Siegel, the American doctor and author of *Love, Medicine and Miracles* says, 'There are no incurable diseases. Only incurable people.'

Statistical diagnosis

Doctors and surgeons work on statistics. They spend days and months reading up material on all sorts of dis-eases, while a few minutes spent talking to the patient suffering the dis-ease could solve the problem. Instead of asking where does it hurt, why don't they ask why does it hurt?

Statistics on the effectiveness of pharmaceutical medication are usually all about tests on animals, their reactions to one pharmaceutical product over another, their rates of healing and death. These results are then related to human beings and it is from information that the patient is treated. Unfortunately in all their tests on animals one major aspect is missing - what was going on within the animal's brain. How does the rat, the mouse or the monkey actually feel while all this suffering is being induced? While doctors read their medical statistics which are all based on behaviourism, testing only what can be observed, they are overlooking the one major factor which has the ability to take away all our dis-ease - the brain.

A further problem with statistical data recorded for the medical profession is that it includes list after list of failed cases, notes on medical reasons why patients didn't pull through after the by-pass, the transplant, the cancer operation. When are they going to keep statistical records on the 'incurable' cases who didn't die? It would be very interesting to find out how many 'incurable' people cured themselves.

There are many records of people who have been 'miraculously' cured. There are people who, by force of mind, have stopped their veins from allowing blood to flow out of their body, when involved in an accident. There are cases where cancer patients have stopped their blood flowing to feed tumours; in this way the tumours were robbed of nourishment and could not grow. There are patients who have been cured by the placebo effect, believing they were receiving pain killers and medication when in fact they were not, but they believed they would get better and so they did get better. There are people who have used the natural formation of endorphins in their brain (a natural opiate) to take pain away. There are instances where patients with a 'fighting spirit' have overcome immense dis-abilities and so-called 'incurable' illness.

You can have a 'life wish' or a 'death wish'. It originates with a thought and the thought is controlled by you. If you want to change negative thoughts you can, with the help of guided imagery.

143

Getting the right image

In order to avail of creative visualisation or guided imagery we have to re-train our sub-conscious to accept new images of our bodies, our capabilities, our financial wealth. There are two essential things to learn in order to achieve successful imagery techniques. The first is to learn or develop the ability for strong mental imagery. The second is to learn how to relax deeply in order to enter our sub-conscious and begin our re-training.

It is the right hemisphere of our brain which holds most of our imagery abilities and, usually, it is this hemisphere which has been neglected since our school days. If you are a parent you will know from experience how your child's imagination had no limitation in the early years, yet with maturity this wonderful ability fades. However, it is easily re-learned and it will only take a few minutes of your time every day to re-train your mind to form positive mental images. The good thing about this re-training is that you can do it anywhere: in the bath, at a bus stop, on a plane, in the supermarket. To begin with, keep your eyes closed while imaging, but as you become more adept you can do it with your eyes open.

First of all, look around you and pick out some object which is simple in design and perhaps just one colour, for instance a coffee mug. Look at its outline and take in its colour. Now, close you eyes and imagine it in your mind. Remember its shape, its handle, its colour. Open your eyes and look at a spoon. See its curve, its shine, its design. Again, close your eyes and imagine the spoon. Now look at the mug and the spoon together. Close your eyes and imagine them both together. When visualising objects remember them in colour. Think of how you feel when you touch them. Is the mug hot to the touch? What does the coffee taste like? Think of the noise the spoon makes when you stir the coffee.

In this way you can build up images of objects in the kitchen, the office environment, a summer garden, the scent of a particular rose, the interior of the car, the noise of the engine, the smell of petrol - the list is endless. The object of this exercise is to 'see' things with your eyes closed.

Now, we have re-trained ourselves to see with our eyes closed that we can show pictures to our sub-conscious and, remember, our sub-conscious cannot tell the difference between a 'real' experience and one that is vividly and repeatedly imagined!

Relaxation techniques

The next step is to get in touch with our sub-conscious. To do this we have to relax our defences, and so the secret is to learn to go into deep relaxation. There are several ways of learning to do this. You can try hypnotherapy to help you relax and the therapist can help you further by implanting a post-hypnotic suggestion in your mind which will help you relax in your own environment. Another way is to buy a cassette of relaxation music, widely available nowadays, and follow the written or verbal instructions which go along with the tape.

You can also teach yourself to relax. Although the following guide looks very long in print, it only takes a few minutes to follow the instructions. You might like to record the instructions yourself and play the tape back, if possible with relaxing, repetitive music playing under it.

First of all, find a quiet environment where you will not be disturbed for at least half an hour. Lie on the floor or the bed, or sit in a comfortable chair. Wherever you choose make sure you are in a comfortable environment wearing comfortable clothing. Cover your lower limbs with a blanket if you wish, and lie or sit with your arms by your sides, your feet apart. Let your jaw fall open a little.

Now, close your eyes and take a long, deep breath. Allow the breath to reach as far into your body as possible. Now slowly exhale. Do this a few times and soon you will feel your heartbeat has slowed down and your breathing has become regular.

The next stage is to concentrate on each separate part of your body, one part at a time. Start with your feet. Say to yourself: I am relaxing my feet. My feet are becoming relaxed. My feet are very relaxed. When your feet have relaxed you then move on to your calves. Again, say to yourself: I am relaxing my calves. My calves are becoming relaxed. My calves are very relaxed.

Follow these instructions all the way up your thighs, your hips, your pelvis, until you come to your neck, your face, your scalp. You are now within your sub-conscious state. Now you can re-train your sub-conscious with a new belief system.

When you have used the techniques of re-training your sub-conscious suggested in the following pages, you can tell your mind to return to its conscious self whenever you want to. Afterwards you will feel relaxed and energetic as though you have had a good sleep!

With practice you will discover that it is easy to come to this state of deep relaxation, breathing deeply and regularly. The more you practise the easier it becomes and you will be able to achieve it on a train, in a plane or even when you are surrounded by people. It is a world you can enter at will and is a perfect release from the stresses of today's environment.

Techniques for imaging health

Blood is the life force within each of us. It feeds every part of us, bringing nourishment and oxygen to every millimetre of our skin and into every organ of our body. Blood regenerates us. As old cells die away new cells are formed with the help of our nourishing blood-stream.

Think of blood as a stream of joy rushing through your body. It courses through your veins to your brain and brings wonderful thoughts. Blood courses to your heart which is filled with joy at the miracle of life. If you love yourself and you love life you won't be able to stop joy flowing through your body. But if you do not love yourself or your life you will lack joy. Blood which lacks joy stops flowing, just as though a switch has been turned off, and so the heart stops beating and seizes up.

However, to practice this now you must love yourself at least a little bit if not a lot, so you can visualise this joyful blood flowing through your body, bringing nourishment and life to new cells. You can use your blood stream to bring health all around your body.

To heal your dis-ease you must first acknowledge it is there. Try to visualise the problem. If it is a skin disorder imagine the tiny blood capillaries under the skin being squeezed too tightly to let the nourishment out to the skin. Now in your mind travel through your blood-stream, up to the top of the capillaries. Once there you can help them unravel themselves so as to reach up to the skin and nourish it once again.

If your knee joint is aching with rheumatism go on that journey down your blood-stream and when you reach the aching joint imagine that you are massaging some healing ointment on to the joint. Go back again and again as often as it needs it.

When you want to get rid of something that is in your blood-stream and damaging your health, bring a miniature vacuum cleaner into your veins and begin to vacuum up the damaging cells. When the bag is full take it out and empty it into the dustbin and put a fresh, empty bag into the vacuum and start again.

When you take medication from your doctor imagine it moving through your blood-stream and give its healing properties a helping hand.

Before you leave this relaxed state, try visualising yourself without the complaint. See yourself up and about, smiling, joyful and active. Never forget that the sub-conscious cannot distinguish between what is 'real' and what is an imagined experience. If it believes the body is healthy it will work hard towards it being healthy. Remember the power of the psyche over the soma (mind over body). Remember the power of your present thought. No one can get into your mind but yourself.

Techniques for imaging material well-being

The very same prognosis applies for physical and material well-being. We cannot change the social and economic system by will-power alone, but we can learn to see and grasp opportunities hidden to us earlier.

No, money will not fall from the skies to make us rich, but if we re-train our sub-conscious to think positively, it can direct us along pathways which can improve the material quality of our lives.

The way to re-train our sub-conscious is to follow the relaxation technique as before and image ourselves in healthy material situations. When we are in our conscious state we will be guided by our re-trained sub-conscious which will take us along the right pathways to bring it about. These new pathways can often be quite surprising. Your sub-conscious, now accepting material well-being, will recognise ways to achieve it. You will suddenly find yourself noticing things you never saw before. You might buy a different newspaper than usual or walk in a different area and suddenly see a job opening which would normally remain unseen by you. You might read an article about a new training scheme for a career you always wanted to get into but never knew the ropes. You might ask a stranger for information and suddenly see a whole new vista opening before you.

The essential thing is to believe differently than before. If you wear drab clothes you will seem a drab person. Imaging is about altering your state of mind - adopting a positive position. There are, of course, social and economic conditions which determine our lives. These are systems which are constructed by society. While imaging alone may not tear down these social and economic constructs, it can allow every woman to adopt a positive attitude when interacting with other individuls. Wearing bright colours will give a new image not just to yourself but to those you come in contact with. Just think for a moment if you were approached by two people, one wearing drab colours, the other bright and cheerful. Who would you prefer to be with?

Imaging success in relationships

The wrong attitude caused by shyness or past bad experiences can cause problems in both business and personal relationships.

However, just because a relationship failed or you didn't succeed in one job does not mean that you will always be a failure. If that were the case no baby would learn to walk, for how often does a child fall before she finds her feet? The same would apply to talking. What child learns to speak perfectly first time around?

The past is just that, passed. What happened last year, last week, an hour ago is the past. It should have no bearing on the present or the future. Remember that you hold the key to your own happiness and success. It is not what happens to you that counts, it is how you respond to it that matters.

Again, follow the relaxation technique as shown earlier. Then imagine yourself in successful situations.

For instance, if you have problems relating to a colleague at work, see instead an image of yourself and that colleague getting on well. See both of you accepting and giving each other support. It may seem an impossible situation to begin with but once you've told your sub-conscious that this is the way it is you will find yourself reacting in a different manner when you meet that colleague.

The same idea applies if you have problems expressing yourself at meetings or in conversations with a superior. Again imagine yourself delivering your report or your message with confidence and being applauded by your superiors. Don't allow niggling thoughts of shyness or ineptitude to enter your subconscious. When you deliver yourself you are always a success. That is the message. Soon you will see yourself expressing your opinions in a confident, relaxed manner. You have reprogrammed yourself to be that way, therefore you are that way.

In personal relationships shyness and past experiences need never get in the way. Relax, use the technique as shown earlier, and see you and a partner getting on well. See yourself in your best light, being affectionate and amusing. See your partner smiling in contentment. Imagine you both suited to each other in mind and body. Then you will find you are being subconsciously directed to look for the right type of partner and, when found, you will act in a manner which will attract that person.

Success does not come about overnight for anyone. It takes time and commitment to succeed but remember you cannot achieve a goal until you set one. Start slowly at first, and soon you will discover you are achieving little goals week by week and then day by day.

Just because you see others around you achieving great heights does not mean that your goals are insignificant or unnecessary. To some even getting on greeting terms with a neighbour may be a huge hurdle. If so, why not begin by a short hand-wave of recognition? That's one barrier down. Now the next time you meet you can smile. That's another goal achieved. What about a short greeting on the third occasion? It can be just 'hello'. Take it step by step. The same rules apply if you want to climb Mount Everest. To get to the top you have to start at the very beginning, at the lowest level. Taken in stages any project can be achieved.

The most important thing to remember is the power of your mind. Remember when it comes to the guidance of your subconscious, seeing is believing. That is the secret of guided imagery.

How to find out more

Hay, Louise L, *You Can Heal Your Life*, Eden Grove Editions, London, 1988.
Shone, Ronald, *Creative Visualisation*, Thorsons, England, 1984.
Siegel, Dr Bernie *Love, Medicine and Miracles*, Arrow New Age, England, 1989.

Chinese Astrology

In China, as in the West, astrology and astronomy were originally linked together. In the year 2,256 BC, at the request of Emperor Yao, the first calendar was calculated in order to advise the population regarding the best time to sow, reap and harvest their crops. (The Emperor was considered a god and had a 'divine right' over the populace.) It was not until around 100 AD that this calendar of the stars began to be used for personal fortune telling.

Nowadays, millions of Chinese all around the world will not make a decision on love, health, business or family life before first consulting their *T'ung Shu*, an almanac which lists astrological and astronomical data for each day of the Chinese Year. If the *T'ung Shu* divines it to be a lucky day then they will stand by their decision, if unlucky they will defer action until advised to do so by the stars. However while Chinese astrology warns of what may happen if we continue along the present path, as with Western astrology we can use our free will to accept our fortune or to change it by our own actions.

Chinese astrology is completely different to Western or Occidental astrology. Firstly, the Chinese calendar is measured in a sixty year cycle, which itself is broken down into five cycles of twelve years, each year represented by a different animal, beginning with the Year of the Rat and ending with the Year of the Pig. Secondly, the Chinese calendar is based on the annual cycle of lunar movement, while the Occidental calendar is based on solar movement as its energy passes through the planets and constellations each year.

The lunar year consists of 12 moons or months, each with 29.5 days. To ensure 'full' days the year is composed of some 29-day-months and some 30-day months. Some years have 7 months of 30 days, others have 5, so the Chinese year differs from the Occidental year by 10-12 days. This explains why the Chinese New Year can fall on any date from 21 January in the Occidental calendar to 20 February. Capricorns and Aquarians need to check carefully for the date of the Chinese New Year in their year of birth in order to find which animal sign they fall under.

Authentic Chinese astrology

The Tzu Wei horoscope

It is easy to discover the animal sign under which we were born, but these animal signs are just one element of the Chinese horoscope. Basically, they can tell us certain elements of our character and with whom we are compatible. However, an authentic Chinese horoscope will tell us in great detail what fortune awaits us, describe our relationship with parents, siblings and colleagues and predict the type of partner we might have, the character of our children, our wealth and property and even what illness will befall us and the years in which significant events may occur.

One of the first recorded systems is known as *Tzu Wei Astrology*. Tzu Wei is the Purple Star or the Pole Star, the centre of the astrological calendar and of Chinese astronomy. The god of birth lives in the Southern Measure and the god of death in the Northern Measure (known to us as Ursa Minor and Ursa Major). At the centre of life is the Pole Star, and all other stars in the Tzu Wei system are there because of their relation to the Pole Star.

A Tzu Wei astrologer needs to know the hour, year and date of your birth. These then need to be changed into the Chinese year and date, which is the first step in divining your personal horoscope. From these dates the next stage is to discover what heavenly stem (star) was in which position in the heavens at the time of your birth. This is then linked with an earthly branch, and so we now have a reading for the relationship of heaven and earth at specific times.

The day of birth corresponds with one of 28 constellations which change every 28 days. This constellation stays with you all your life. The constellations are also named after animals such as the crocodile, badger, fox, leopard, wolf, cock, etc. but these are not associated with the animals of the twelve years. They are, however, associated with the five elements: wood, fire, earth, metal and water and with the four seasons.

The time of our birth is essential for a full and correct Tzu

Wei horoscope to be cast. Again there is a major difference between this and the Occidental horoscope, because in China the time span differs - there are only twelve 'hours' in a Chinese day, each of which is equivalent to two Occidental hours. From knowing our hour of birth it is also possible to discover a basic prediction, covering suitable career choices, unlucky ages and even the probable year of our death!

Now we know that the Tzu Wei or Pole Star astrological system is the relationship between the heavenly stems (the stars) and their earthly branches (the earth). But there is one element missing to form a triangle, and that is us, because humanity is also an integral part of the universe. The interaction of heaven and earth is made through us and we are responsible for the harmony between Yin and Yang, light and dark, heaven and earth. It is through our actions that we can maintain or upset the harmonious balance of the universe. Once we know what lies in store it is up to us to ensure balance through thoughtful action. When we have a map of our fortune in our hands we are free to choose our own pathway.

The Tzu Wei horoscope goes into great depth and many calculations are required to tell someone's fortune. The following is a 'westernised' way of using Chinese astrology in its simplest form.

Simplified Chinese astrology

The legend of Buddha and the animals of the earth
Although the Chinese horoscope pre-dates Buddha, legend has it that one day many centuries ago, Buddha called the animals of the earth to him in order to pass on to them his infinite knowledge. Few animals answered his call, and those who did had to brave the waters of a fast-running river to cross to the bank by which Buddha waited. Buddha promised that the first animal to reach him would be honoured by having its name on the first year of the Chinese calendar. Some were side-tracked on the way, allowing their natural curiosity to way-lay them, others like the snake dozed for a while, and were overtaken by the more ambitious.

When the animals arrived at the river bank they saw it was swift-flowing. The rat knew it would drown if it were to attempt to swim across it, but its ambition made it determined to get to the other side. Always an opportunist, it climbed on to the back of the ox whose steady strength carried them both safely to the opposite bank. Just before the ox reached the bank, the rat leaped from its back on to the land and so was the first to reach Buddha who, true to his promise, named the first year after it.

The slow-moving but determined ox arrived next, never for a moment deviating from its objective. The tiger followed the ox, a little delayed by its mistrusting instinct which caused it to often pause and sniff the air for danger. After the ox came the hare moving quickly but carefully through the undergrowth.

The powerful, eye-catching dragon was a little delayed because it had to stop awhile to bask in the attention of those it met along the way who admired its shiny, glittering body. The snake, often so quick to act, paused for a snooze in the warm grass, but thereafter used its charms to discover the shortest route to the opposite bank. The horse came next, quick and nimble on its feet but shying away at the slightest interruption, followed by the ram, not so nimble but always landing on its feet.

The next to arrive was the fast-talking, quick-thinking monkey, who nevertheless lost time because it just had to stop once too often for a chat. After it came the cock, delayed by its ever-present need to search for crumbs and grit along the wayside. The dog followed, busy guarding against enemies and stopping now and then to worry a bone, and last but not least came the pig, content just to arrive at its destination at last, not caring for the rush and thrust of the competition.

So this is how, according to legend, these twelve animals were chosen to characterise the attitudes and behaviour of the twelve different years within the Chinese cycle. It is important to note that in other Eastern countries the ox is known as the buffalo, the hare is known as the cat or the rabbit, the ram is known as the sheep or the goat, the cock is known as the rooster and the pig is known as the boar.

Finding your sign
The following table gives the dates for the full sixty-year cycle showing the corresponding animal sign. Capricorns and Aquarians should take special note of the dates of the last day and the first day of the new years.

Table of the Chinese signs

THE RAT	THE OX	THE TIGER
31.1.1900/18.2.1901	19.2.1901/ 7.2.1902	8.2.1902/28.1.1903
18.2.1912/ 5.2.1913	6.2.1913/25.1.1914	26.1.1914/13.2.1915
5.2.1924/24.1.1925	25.1.1925/12.2.1926	13.2.1926/ 1.2.1927
24.1.1936/10.2.1937	11.2.1937/30.1.1938	31.1.1938/18.2.1939
10.2.1948/28.1.1949	29.1.1949/16.2.1950	17.2.1950/ 5.2.1951
28.1.1960/14.2.1961	15.2.1961/ 4.2.1962	5.2.1962/24.1.1963
15.2.1972/ 2.2.1973	3.2.1973/22.1.1974	23.1.1974/10.2.1975
2.2.1984/19.2.1985	20.2.1985/ 8.2.1986	9.2.1986/28.1.1987

THE RABBIT	THE DRAGON	THE SNAKE
29.1.1903/15.2.1904	16.2.1904/ 3.2.1905	4.2.1905/24.1.1906
14.2.1915/ 2.2.1916	3.2.1916/22.1.1917	23.1.1917/10.2.1918
2.2.1927/22.1.1928	23.1.1928/ 9.2.1929	10.2.1929/29.1.1930
19.2.1939/ 7.2.1940	8.2.1940/26.1.1941	27.1.1941/14.2.1942
6.2.1951/26.1.1952	27.1.1952/13.2.1953	14.2.1953/ 2.2.1954
25.1.1963/12.2.1964	13.2.1964/ 1.2.1965	2.2.1965/20.1.1966
11.2.1975/30.1.1976	31.1.1976/17.2.1977	18.2.1977/ 6.2.1978
29.1.1987/16.2.1988	17.2.1988/ 5.2.1989	6.2.1989/26.1.1990

THE HORSE	THE GOAT	THE MONKEY
25.1.1906/12.2.1907	13.2.1907/ 1.2.1908	2.2.1908/21.1.1909
11.2.1918/31.1.1919	1.2.1919/19.2.1920	20.2.1920/ 7.2.1921
30.1.1930/16.2.1931	17.2.1931/ 5.2.1932	6.2.1932/25.1.1933
15.2.1942/ 4.2.1943	5.2.1943/24.1.1944	25.1.1944/12.2.1945
3.2.1954/23.1.1955	24.1.1955/11.2.1956	12.2.1956/30.1.1957
21.1.1966/ 8.2.1967	9.2.1967/28.1.1968	29.1.1968/16.2.1969
7.2.1978/27.1.1979	28.1.1979/15.2.1980	16.2.1980/ 4.2.1981
27.1.1990/14.2.1991	15.2.1991/ 3.2.1992	4.2.1992/22.1.1993

THE ROOSTER	THE DOG	THE PIG
22.1.1909/ 9.2.1910	10.2.1910/29.1.1911	30.1.1911/17.2.1912
8.2.1921/27.1.1922	28.1.1922/15.2.1923	16.2.1923/ 4.2.1924
26.1.1933/13.2.1934	14.2.1934/ 3.2.1935	4.2.1935/23.1.1936
13.2.1945/ 1.2.1946	2.2.1946/21.1.1947	22.1.1947/ 9.2.1948
31.1.1957/15.2.1958	16.2.1958/ 7.2.1959	8.2.1959/27.1.1960
17.2.1969/ 5.2.1970	6.2.1970/26.1.1971	27.1.1971/14.2.1972
5.2.1981/24.1.1982	25.1.1982/12.2.1983	13.2.1983/ 1.2.1984
23.1.1993/ 9.2.1994	10.2.1994/30.1.1995	31.1.1995/18.2.1996

Character and destiny of each sign

In China each of the animals of the horoscope is looked upon in a totally different manner than in the West, so if you discover that you are a Rat or a Snake, don't have an identity crisis - each is honoured in its own way and to be a Snake is considered the most admirable of all!

The following is an outline description of the traits of each of the animals. Obviously, when studied in depth the character of a Rat born at 5 am on 3 February will have many contrasting features to the Rat born at 8 pm on 30 August, and so on.

The Rat
The most ambitious and aggressive of the signs, the Rat always wants to be first and will use all her wiles to get there. On the outside she is charming and sophisticated, but she really likes to burrow deep into the secrets of the earth and will rarely confide her plans or her problems to anyone. She needs to be active both physically and mentally, and will worry anxiously about having enough stores to keep her in the future.

The Rat is the most intelligent of the signs, and she should use her intellect to remember that she is destined for the trap. It would, therefore, be best for her to work alone and stay single, at least until she has achieved her career goals.

Compatible with the Rat, the Ox, the Dragon, the Monkey and the Dog. Avoid the Horse and the Hare.

The Ox
The Ox works slowly and steadily with deep commitment in order to make the earth fertile. She is self-sufficient and likes to be alone to think and to work out the most balanced way to achieve her goals. With a strong, able back, the Ox often finds others lean quite heavily on her for support, but she is usually willing to help.

Her placid exterior often hides a stubborn intolerance of others, and she is rather an authoritarian, bellowing and stomping in order to get her voice heard. However, these rages are rare, and the Ox would much prefer to work hard and create beautiful things, usually connected with the earth.

Compatible with the Rat, the Hare, the Snake and the Rooster. Avoid the Tiger, the Goat and the Monkey.

The Tiger
The Tiger is the chief of the jungle in China, and she has all the traits of the chief: loyal, courageous and generous on one hand, imprudent, selfish and rebellious on the other.

It is this need for attention at all costs which can bring the Tiger down. While standing courageously for what she thinks is right she will not back down, even when she knows she is wrong. She would do well to learn to trust others and their judgement on occasion for, with a little more forethought and a little less pride the Tiger can go far and make a lot of money.

Compatible with the Horse, the Dragon and the Dog. Avoid the Snake, the Monkey and the Ox.

The Hare

The Hare, also known as the Rabbit or the Cat, should not be restrained in small confines but allowed to roam far and free.

The Hare will always land on her feet and, knowing this, is a happy-go-lucky person who is fun to be around. Loving company and the good things of life such as a warm hearth, good food and beautiful surroundings, the Hare can be very welcoming. But don't be surprised if she proves to be a rather superficial friend if the boat is rocked because, above all else, her own security must come first; it is essential to her.

Compatible with the Ox, the Snake, the Goat, the Monkey, the Dog and the Pig. Avoid the Tiger, the Hare and the Cock.

The Dragon

The Dragon is the symbol of power, of the glittering, fire-breathing, many-headed beast of fable whose lair is hidden deep within mountains where she guards magnificent treasure. The Dragon's mystique is in her mystery and magnificence, and she turns many a head who stops to admire her glittering coat of armour.

Full of enthusiasm, vitality and heady schemes, the Dragon is gifted and generous. She likes to breathe fire into projects, but don't hold your breath waiting for her to see it through. Her major fault is that, she will rarely fulfil her promise.

Compatible with the Rat, the Snake, the Monkey and the Rooster. Avoid the Dog and the Tiger.

The Snake

This is the symbol of the Kundalini Snake, whose energies intermingle psychic and mental abilities, arousing paranormal and spiritual powers. For this reason the Snake is the most revered sign in the Chinese Zodiac.

The Snake is considered the most charming, beautiful and sexually attractive of the signs. Well-groomed and well-dressed, Snakes will see any task through to its conclusion, and are usually lucky in money matters. They make good friends but rather unfaithful partners. Snakes are capable of quick action when required, but prefer to conserve their energy, lying quietly in the sun, and thinking deeply.

Compatible with the Ox, the Hare, the Dragon and the Rooster. Avoid the Tiger and the Pig.

The Horse
The Horse symbolises the most noble of beasts. She can be the hardest worker in the field or the most fickle; she can carry the heaviest load over rugged mountains and through raging torrents yet shies away from the flames of a fire.

While you can admire the outward character of the Horse, no one can really fathom her depths. She is quick-witted, hot blooded, hot tempered, entertaining and popular. Her desire to be a winner makes her selfish, and she will trample anyone who gets in her way. However, she will work hard and her ability to handle money will be to everyone's benefit.

Compatible with the Goat, the Dog and the Tiger. Avoid the Rat, the Monkey and the Cock.

The Ram
In the eyes of the Ram the grass is always greener in the next field. She is very active and constantly in motion, so it's just as well she is so adaptable to any environment. The Ram is easily led, yet when she gets a strong message from her intuition she can really dig her heels in and remain unmovable on certain points. Elegant and charming the Ram will always land on her feet, sometimes using the backs of others to break her fall.

The Ram lives in a state of anxiety and makes constant demands for reassurance from her colleagues and friends. She would make a good writer or artist, but a bad trader. She loves living in a peaceful world surrounded by beautiful possessions, which of course will have been provided by someone else.

Compatible with the Hare, the Pig and the Horse. Avoid the Dog, the Goat and the Ox.

The Monkey
This is the sign of ingenuity and quick-thinking, intuition and creativity. It can also be the sign of opportunism and dishonesty!

The Monkey is always active, playful and sociable, quick to learn both mentally and physically and, so long as she can keep her attention on the task in hand, she will always succeed. Keeping her attention on the project in hand is her greatest

157

problem for, although the Monkey is deft and able for all things, she hates to miss out on anything that's going on around her. This charming animal can get in to places barred to others and quickly extricate herself when trouble looms!

Compatible with the Dragon, the Snake, the Pig, the Rat and the Ox. Avoid the Tiger and the Rooster.

The Cock

Also known as the Rooster or the Chicken, the Cock always has to make herself heard and it is important for her to rule the roost.

Full of enthusiasm, the Cock greets each dawn with joy and in her haste to tell others of the wonders of the world she often ignores the need for diplomacy. The Cock is honest and courageous, but sometimes in her wish to speak frankly she can hurt others.

The Cock displays her true brilliance in social situations and makes for stimulating company. If she can stop dreaming of castles in the air, she has the ability to build wealth, and her willingness to share her good fortune with others makes her a good friend and parent.

Compatible with the Ox, the Snake and the Dragon. Avoid the Hare and the Ram.

The Dog

The Dog makes a wonderful friend and companion, faithful, loyal and true, generous to the needs of others. On the other hand she is anxious, always on the watch for disasters, and tending to waste time worrying at bones.

The Dog tends to be introverted and secretive, docile to others' demands during the day-time but baying mysteriously at the moon at night. On the outside willing to wag her tail to please others, she won't let go if she feels an injustice has been done. The Dog is a perfect employee who will obey all the rules and work for the good of others, guiding miscreants back to the straight and narrow, guarding newcomers and the less assertive against dangers. Her intelligence will be admired and she will inspire confidence and loyalty in others.

Compatible with the Snake, the Horse, the Hare, the Dog and the Pig. Avoid the Tiger, the Dragon and the Ram.

The Pig

The Pig was the symbol of spirituality in Celtic times and in the

Christian era that of the destroyer.

The Pig is easy-going and slow to anger unless her brood is threatened. Because she enjoys a quiet, unquestioning life, she tends to fall in easily with others' plans. This, however, can prove her downfall because the Pig's own sincerity and honesty doesn't let her see that the hand that feeds her is the same hand that takes her to market.

In order to enjoy a long, fulfilling life, the Pig must make her own decisions and create her own independence.

Compatible with the Tiger, the Hare, the Monkey, the Rooster, the Dog and the Pig. Avoid the Ox, the Dragon, the Snake and the Ram.

How to find out more

Man-Ho, Kwok, *Authentic Chinese Horoscopes*, Arrow Books, London, 1987. (One book on each of the Chinese Signs)
Delsol, Paula, *Chinese Horoscopes*, Pan Books, London, 1973.
Chinese Zodiac Signs, Omnibus Edition. Treasure Press, London, 1988. (original text in French by Catherine Aubier, translated by Eileen Finletter and Ian Murray)